Serve

in

Spirit

Serve

in

Spirit

WATCHMAN NEE

CHRISTIAN FELLOWSHIP PUBLISHERS, INC.
NEW YORK

SERVE IN SPIRIT

ISBN 13: 978-0-935008-89-0
ISBN 10: 0-935008-89-6

Original Limited Print Edition, April 2009
Reprint Edition, October 2009

Note: The contents of this Reprint Edition is fundamentally the same as the Original Limited Edition printed earlier this year, but with some necessary additional editing added for clarity and easier understanding.

Any further reprintings of the book hereafter will likewise reflect this additional editing.

Available from the Publishers at:

11515 Allecingie Parkway
Richmond, Virginia 23235
www.c-f-p.com

Printed in the United States of America

FOREWORD

"God is my witness, whom I serve in my spirit in the gospel of his Son, how unceasingly I make mention of you, always in my prayers" (Rom. 1.9). This is the testimony of the apostle Paul. Should this not be true for all who are called to serve? God is Spirit, and He can only be served in spirit, not in flesh. Although this sounds simple, it is a fundamental principle of service that is being violated all the time. How we need to be reminded again and again lest we forget.

At the First Training Conference in 1948[*] God's servant Watchman Nee gave a series of messages on "The Breaking of the Outward Man and the Release of the Spirit." These messages were published in Chinese in May 1955 and were translated and published in English under the title of *The Release of the Spirit* in 1965. Due to the extreme importance of the subject matter Watchman Nee reiterated it at the Second Training Conference in 1949. The notes to these messages were recently discovered. We recall what God's word has said: "God speaketh once, yea twice, though man regardeth it not" (Job 33.14). God knows our frailty, so He speaks once and twice. We certainly need such precious repetitions; hence, the present translation and publication into English of these notes. The

---

[*] This is a reference to the Training Conferences for fellow workers convened by brother Nee during the summers of 1948 and 1949 that were held on Mount Kuling not far inland from the port city of Fuzhou (known then as Foochow) in the southern Chinese province of Fujian (known then as Fukien).

reader will find that though the basic thoughts are the same in both series of messages, the way of expression varies.

Furthermore, at the same time we also obtained the notes taken from Watchman Nee's instructions on service presented to the young people in Shanghai, spoken in January 1949. Like the apostle Paul, brother Nee always had the young people in heart. These are valuable instructions to young believers who have a heart to serve, and they are given as the second part of the present volume.

May the God whom we serve truly be better served by all who love Him.

Scripture quotations are from the
American Standard Version of the Bible
(1901), unless otherwise indicated.

Serve in Spirit

Part One:
Serve in Spirit

"God is my witness, whom I serve in my spirit in the gospel of his Son, how unceasingly I make mention of you, always in my prayers."

Romans 1.9

Chapter 1

SERVE IN SPIRIT

"God is my witness, whom I serve in my spirit in the gospel of his Son." (Rom. 1.9a)

A person who serves God must sooner or later learn to use his spirit. How often he finds himself being torn between two opposite forces: the inward and the outward. He is thus unable to yield to the discipline of the Holy Spirit but is controlled by an opposite, outward force. The greatest problem in service is the outward man, which inhibits the exercise of the spirit. One should use his spirit to touch the spirit of the other person. However, due to the inhibition caused by the outward man, his spirit cannot be released. The outward man prevents the inward spirit from functioning. For this reason, without the basic dealing of the outward man, one cannot even serve rightly. The dealing of the outward man, therefore, is most foundational.

"So then I of myself with the mind [or, the inward man] ... serve the law of God; but with the flesh [or, the outward man] the law of sin" (Rom. 7.25b). "That he would grant you, according to the riches of his glory, that ye may be strengthened with power through his Spirit in the inward man" (Eph. 3.16). "Wherefore we faint not; but though our outward man is decaying, yet our inward man is renewed day by day" (2 Cor. 4.16).

That part of a person in which God dwells is the inward man; the rest of the person is the outward man. The regenerated spirit of man is the inward man; his soulical faculties the outward man. The inward man is clothed with the outward man. God's own Spirit, life and power are all in the inward part of man. How greatly do the thoughts, emotions and volitions of the outward man interfere and inhibit the inward man!

In order to serve God the inward man must be able to launch out. The basic difficulty lies in how the inward man can thrust through the outward man. The former has been imprisoned for quite a long time and unless it be released, there is no effective work which can be done. The bondage of the inward man creates a serious problem. In fact, nothing interferes with the work of God more than this. The outward man must be broken so that God may be manifested, the inward man may come forth, and God's work may be done. This is an essential matter, for burden is in the spirit. Herein is the issue.

John 12.24 tells us: "Verily, verily, I say unto you, Except a grain of wheat fall into the earth and die, it abideth by itself alone; but if it die, it beareth much fruit." Unless a grain of wheat dies it cannot bear fruit, for life is in the grain of wheat. It falls into the earth and after its shell is cracked open, it buds. Various elements in the earth work on the grain, causing it to break so that life is released.

The Scriptures state plainly that whoever loves his soul life shall lose it (see Matt. 16.25, Mark 8.35, Luke 9.24). The outer shell is a man's own life, whereas the life within is the life of the Lord. Without the breaking of the outward, the inward cannot be released. In the world there are the dead and the living. (The dead are those who do not have the life of God; the living are those who have God's life). Similarly, within the church there are those whose life in them is inhibited and those whose life within is released. In the latter the Lord has broken through and found His way out. Today the problem lies not in getting life but in getting the life out. It takes many years to break down self. This is not mere word or doctrine.

All things are possible with the Lord, but the life is locked in us. Without the breaking of the outward man people will not be blessed, for the Lord himself is being blocked. The pure nard is truly spiritual but it is locked in the alabaster cruse. Unless the alabaster cruse is broken the pure nard has no way to pour forth. Nonetheless, many deem the outward man to be much more valuable than the inward man. How we treasure our own clever ideas, warm emotions and accurate opinions. All in the house are waiting to see the smashing of the alabaster cruse, waiting to smell the fragrance of the pure nard. But if the alabaster cruse is not broken, how can the pure nard be released? (see Mark 14.3ff.) During all these years the Holy Spirit has not ceased working. All of the disciplines of God upon us are for one purpose: the breaking of our outward man. The Lord himself provides the way. Sadly, some are unwilling to go this way of the cross, and thus have dropped out.

From the time we are saved the Lord is constantly working one thing in us: the breaking down of the outward man. For what the world needs is the treasure, not the earthen vessel. Unless the earthen vessel is broken the treasure is not released (cf. 2 Cor. 4.7). Yet because the way of blessing is stained with blood, how few are traveling on this road! The fearful and the cautious will never experience the breaking of the outward man. Only the committed are ready to be broken. Each and every one of us must come to recognize the purpose of the Lord's dealings in our lives. All the things which one experiences during his lifetime are full of meaning. For the sake of breaking our outward man, whatever experiences the Lord may give us are always the best, the best of heaven. Every day's happenings are catered towards the breaking of the outward man. Ordinarily, it will take quite a number of years for it to be broken.

The Lord uses two different methods to break the outward man: one is accumulative in character and the other is sudden. To some He gives sudden breaking and then accumulative dealings; to others He first uses daily or accumulative dealings and then sudden breaking. Although we are not able to shorten the time of breaking, we certainly can lengthen its time. How very regretful is the waste of time. The church is not revived and the loss to God is great. Let us therefore come to God with one accord to offer ourselves absolutely to Him. Let us put ourselves in His hand for the sake of the spiritual future of the church.

What is meant by the "cross"? The cross is the brokenness of the outward man (see John 12.24). Make no mistake, he who thinks of preserving himself intact has no spiritual future. This path of the cross is well marked. The breaking of the outward man for the use of the spirit — such is the way of the cross. Brother T. Austin-Sparks was a man whose mind was clear, whose will was strong, and whose feeling was deep; yet those who met him met his spirit, a pure spirit. Miss Margaret E. Barber was a quick person yet all who met her touched her spirit, not her quickness. We must not let the years of God's dealing in our lives be wasted. Some may be broken, but some cannot be broken due to their self-love. The love of self renders the work of the Lord in one's life fruitless.

The first and foremost difficulty nowadays is that we dwell in darkness and are thus unable to see God's hand. God is working; God is doing the work of breaking, yet men fail to see that He is trying to break them. All they see is wrong treatment or bad environment. They have no light, they do not see God's hand. May God give us a revelation that the hand on us is not that of any family member or any brother or sister, but the hand of God. May we learn to say from our hearts, "What the Lord does, I humbly accept."

The second difficulty is "self-love." May God get rid of our self-love. Seeing that it is God's hand, may I also be willing to add my hand to it. All misunderstandings, all fretfulnesses, and all discontentments come from self-love, the love of saving oneself. Trying to preserve oneself is the cause of all these problems. It is like someone longing for the wine mingled with gall after having ascended the cross. Our Lord drank only one cup — the Father's cup; not the second cup — the cup of wine mingled with gall (see Matt. 26.39,27.33-4).

O Lord! All is Yours. You aim at breaking the outward man. How my self-love resists You. Today I once again deliver myself into Your hand.

He who has been broken by God is most beautiful. In the Old Testament Isaac and Jacob illustrate this contrast. One was naturally good and the other was naturally bad. However, when Isaac and Jacob reached their old age, Isaac's eyes were dim so that he could not see; but Jacob, after he had been dealt with by God, being stricken again and again, had his spiritual eyes opened wide, and worshiped leaning upon the top of his staff at his death (see Heb. 11.21). In the entire Bible, who is worse than Jacob? Yet at the time of his death none rises higher than he. After scores of years of being broken, the final outcome is altogether lovely. So, this is the only way for us. Nothing is more lovely than to see God manifested in human life. The Lord expects to see wounds, to see scars by which the Spirit is released. Praise the Lord!*

---

* Note: Message given on April 13, 1949.

Chapter 2

BREAKING OF THE OUTWARD MAN

The breaking of the outward man is the primary and foundational experience of a worker, for only after brokenness will there be effective work. For an unbroken person there are two possibilities. Firstly, since his spirit is not released, he works by his natural mind and emotions. Due to the inhibition of the spirit, such work cannot cause people to meet God. The second possibility is that though the worker's spirit may be released, it is nonetheless clothed with his own feeling, affection and thought; therefore, the expression of the spirit is mixed and impure. Under either of these two possibilities no effective work is accomplished. The key to effective work is to have the basic understanding that it is the spirit rather than thought and feeling that gives life. How very true is God's word. Many have to be brought by God to their end before they can see that "the spirit giveth life" (2 Cor. 3.6b). Many must go through many failures before their spirits are released to bring sinners to regeneration and believers to edification. Without spiritual words there will not be regeneration or edification.

According to God's word, He has no intention to separate His Spirit from our spirit. In fact, many times "spirit" in the Bible cannot be distinguished as to whether it refers to God's Spirit or to man's spirit. In fact, throughout the centuries those who have translated the Bible have had no way to differentiate the word "spirit" in

Romans chapter 8 where that word occurs most. There is no way to decipher whether the word "spirit" refers to God's Spirit or man's spirit. However, this in no way obscures the meaning of the passage, for when we receive the "new spirit" it is also the time we receive the "Holy Spirit." There is no way to separate them. So, when the spirit is released, it is the Holy Spirit who launches out through man's spirit. There *is* a difference, but there is no way to separate them. When the spirit is released, the Holy Spirit too is released. When the normal spirit of man is touched, the Spirit of God is also being touched.

In this matter God has no intention to cause His Spirit to contact man directly. In God's work He always chooses man's spirit to carry Him forth. It is like the electric wire which carries electricity. God has chosen the church to "carry" God's Spirit to men. However, if thought has not been broken, thought will become a hindrance; if emotion has not been broken, emotion will be a blockage. All the redeemed have the Holy Spirit in them; but if anyone is not broken, what is in him cannot be released. Oftentimes the outside is fervent, yet the inside is cold. This is the first condition. On the other hand, there are many times when the inward man is fervent but the outward man remains uncooperative. This is the second condition. In both cases outward thought is independent because the outer shell has not been broken. So, the point of emphasis, the basic lesson to learn is, that before God's work can be done, the inward man must break through the outward and that man's own thought and emotion must not act independently. Otherwise, the work will be fruitless. The breaking of the outward man is therefore the primary objective for one who serves. We aim at finding the way to brokenness. And after being broken, all those outward independent actions will naturally come to an end. We will not perform any longer, neither will our outward man refuse to comply, nor our thought be defective.

The Lord uses the discipline as well as the enlightening of the Holy Spirit to break down the outward man in order to release the spirit. The releasing of the spirit affects not only the work but also the life of the person.

A person whose spirit has been released is able to continue in the presence of God regardless of temporal surroundings; he is also able to touch the Spirit of revelation in the Bible, to receive revelation from God, and to use his spirit to send forth God's word (as a minister of the word). One who has had such dealings is also able to use the spirit to touch another's spirit, to discern another's real spiritual condition, and to make it easy for his own spirit to be touched by others. Although it is difficult for those who are thick-shelled to be touched in their inward man, those who know God are still able to touch them. It is your openness that causes your spirit to flow.

He whose spirit is set free may live continuously in the presence of God. During the second year of my believing the Lord, and after I had read brother Lawrence's *Practicing the Presence of God*, I felt miserable because I was not able to live continuously before God. When we were young in the Lord, for two or three years we prayed frequently in order to return to God to have His presence. For without returning to God we lost His presence. When I was a young believer, I used my memory to maintain myself in the presence of God. This was because I did not know the breaking of the outward man. He who is ignorant of such breaking can never understand the presence of God, for He is Spirit. Only our spirit is of the same makeup, and our spirit alone can enjoy God's presence. Whoever tries to hold on to His presence with his thought and feeling can never maintain it for long. It takes the same nature for two distinct things of that nature to commingle together — such as water with water and air with air. With the breaking of the outward man our spirit is commingled with God's Spirit, and naturally "the presence" will come.

Having the outward man broken, the inward man will no longer be disturbed before God. That which hinders the presence of God is the outward man, for it is the latter that is affected by outside things. The spirit of man responds to the Spirit of God, whereas the outward man reflects the things outside. Although we cannot get rid of outside things, we can break the outward man. While the latter remains intact we are not able to enjoy the presence of God. Hence the enjoyment of God's presence is based on the outward man being broken. As soon as it is broken, the spirit is freed from outside disturbance and thus is able to enjoy the continuous presence of God. Brother Lawrence was a military man who served in the kitchen. He said, "Just as I enjoy the presence of God in my time of prayer, so equally I enjoy His presence in the midst of the clashing of the military plates."

God delivers us from all outside reactions. When the outward man is broken, the organ to react against outside actions is disabled. As a result, one whose outward man is broken has no need to return to God, for the spirit is always in His presence. A broken person neither goes out nor returns back. On the other hand, for an unbroken person, even working can cause him to wander away. He who knows God has no such motions of leaving and returning, for God is in him, and he is in God. Such drifting away is the result of the unbrokenness of the outward man. So as we come before God in this unbroken state, we may indeed sense His presence but later, after we do a little work, we feel we have wandered away. The sensations experienced while being before God and after doing some work are different. Whenever there is this sense of returning, it tells us that we have already drifted away. But once there is the breaking of the outward man there is no need to return to God, for we are now enjoying His presence at all times.

The anger of man is the rudest of his emotions, while the kindness of man is the tenderest of his feelings. To be angry is close to sin, though some angers are not sins. In fact, sometimes, a worker needs to reprove his brethren strongly before God. It is relatively easier to be kind than to be angry. However, even in such situations as the latter, some who know the breaking of the outward man may continue in God's presence without their spirit being disturbed at all. As they reprimand their brethren they still enjoy the presence of God. There is no need for them to return to Him. For with the breaking of the outward man, the inward man is separated from the outward, and thus his inward man may still enjoy God's presence. Outside things can only affect the outward man; they cannot influence the inward man. Yet before brokenness, as outside things touch the outward man, the latter can impede the inward man. But with the breaking of the outward man, he can do things outwardly and yet his inward man enjoys the presence of God as usual: he still lives before God. A worker needs rest for his body, but his spirit needs no recuperation. With the separation of the inward from the outward man he can use the one to conduct business and the other to live before God. Without such separation his entire being will be involved in conducting business; therefore, he needs to pray to return back to God's presence. But with the separation, his outward man may be involved in business, yet his inward man continues to live in the presence of God. When he serves God, his spirit will launch out to help people.

The separation of the outward from the inward man may sometimes look like two lives lived simultaneously. What the outward man does has no effect upon the inward man; for even while the outward man does outside things, the inward man lives before God continually.[*]

---

[*] Note: Message given on April 14, 1949.

Chapter 3

LIMITATION OF THE OUTWARD MAN

Whether a man's spirit is usable for God's work depends no only on the breaking of the outward man but also on the separation of the spirit and the soul — which is the separation of the inward and the outward man. Only after the Spirit of God has accomplished both works will the spirit be usable. "Breaking" and "dividing" are two separate things. Dividing is through revelation, breaking is by the discipline of the Holy Spirit. These two are different. Their workings and objectives vary. We must not treat them as one.

The Thing in Hand

Now concerning preoccupation or the things in hand, suppose a father commands his son to do something, but the son — having already something in hand — asks his father to wait until he finishes his own work. There is already a work in the son's hand before the work of the father. Everybody has something in hand. When God tries to find man to serve Him, man always has something in hand to do. Along the path of God, the thing in hand usually stands in the way, for before God speaks our hands are already full. As long as the outward man is unbroken, we always have many things in hand, and these things hinder us from being spiritually useful. The difficulty lies in the fact that because the outward man has its own things to do, we are not able to respond to the moving of God's

Spirit in us. The Father says to you, "Son, do this for Me," and you reply, "Wait till I finish my thing in hand, then I will come and do Your bidding." Yet the thing in hand is not the thing of the Father. To illustrate further, suppose I can only carry fifty pounds; there is no way to add ten more. Fifty pounds I can carry, but sixty I cannot manage. This fifty pounds is the thing in hand. I am a person with limitation, I cannot do things unlimitedly. Our outward man is like the physical man that has strength, but limited strength. Love is also a function of the outward man. The strength of love is limited just as physical strength is. Should one love his parents to the uttermost, he has no more love left for others.

People have a basic understanding that their physical strength is limited. However, they do not know that the strength of the outward man is also limited. For this reason, many attempts at work are in reality but a waste of strength. People do not recognize that the things in hand are hindrances. Loving one's spouse with one's whole heart leaves no more room to love the brethren and the sinners. There is a limit in human love. After it is exhausted there will be no more left for others. May we pay attention to this fact. In like manner, the strength of our thinking is also limited. No one can think inexhaustibly. If you spend very much time in thinking over a certain matter, you will find yourself unable to think of other things later on.

It is said in Romans 8.2 that "the law of the Spirit of life in Christ Jesus made me free from the law of sin and of death." How important is this statement that the law of the Spirit of life sets me free from the law of sin and of death.

Yet why is it that this is ineffective in some people? Why is it that after many years of preaching, so few are profited? Within what kind of man will the righteousness of God be accomplished? It is the spiritual man: it is the one who minds the things of the Spirit. A spiritual man is under the law of the Holy Spirit and thus has righteousness in him. Such a person is set free from the law of sin and of death and is able to mind the things of the Spirit. How very important it is to be able to mind the things of the Spirit. Who, then, is he who can mind the things of the Spirit? He who does not mind the things of the flesh (see Rom. 8.5ff.).

Clear understanding of this matter is essential. Suppose a mother should leave the care of her child to a neighbor, asking that they please take care of her child. This taking care means that as soon as the child cries, they are to care for him. It does not mean ignoring his cry for half a day. It also means to pay attention to his crawling, sitting or falling. Our attention is limited, our minding is restricted. We cannot mind two things at the same time. One cannot take care of both a child and sheep and cattle at the same time. Only those who are not minding things of the flesh are able to mind the things of the Spirit. Man's mind is limited; it can only center on one thing at a time. "Minding" the Spirit is turning your mind to think only of things spiritual, thus not paying attention to things of the flesh. Unfortunately, it can also be the reverse. However, it cannot be both, due to the limitation of our mind.

Now is the time to use our mind on the things of the Spirit; otherwise, we will be left behind in offering effective service to God. Many err in having too many things in their two hands. In their emotion they have love as the thing in hand; in their mind they are filled with thoughts. They have exhausted their thinking strength so that they cannot be minded of anything else. Having only limited strength in their shoulders, they are unable to carry more weight. As the things in hand increase, the things of God decrease. If a person has his emotion and mind fully occupied, he will be too exhausted to answer God's call. God has to wait two days for his emotion and mind to recover before He can even speak to him. We must realize that our limitation is the problem, a very serious problem.

Some may have a strong will. They appear so strong as though they have unlimited will power. But when they have to make a decision before God, they waver and vacillate. They may seem to be strong in will, but they are extremely weak in using their will in the things of God. Some may have many ideas and opinions. But in finding the will of God they are totally confused and utterly perplexed. This is because their hands are so filled with outside things that their outward man has used up all its strength so that there is no more strength to spare.

How very limited is the outward man. Whenever there is a thing in hand, the outward man is restricted and the spirit is also restrained. The Spirit will not bypass our spirit and work; and our spirit must also work through the outward man. When the latter is occupied with the thing in hand, the spirit of man loses its access and God's Spirit is blocked. Therefore, the outward man must be broken, otherwise God will be bound.

The thing in hand has its peculiar nature. It is never the thing of God. All the things in hand are things independent of Him. They are non-compliant towards God. He must break our things in hand before we can love the brethren. Before God can move, all the things which are in hand need to be broken, so that His love may come forth. The breaking of the outward man is absolutely necessary. If there be things in hand in our will, then God will have to strike heavily till we dare not ask or act. Our will must be totally submissive before God can use our will. Unless the outward man is usable, the inward man is unable to do its work. There may indeed be work in the spirit, but there is no mouth to be used. At Pentecost, there were words as well as utterance. If man's word is missing, then God's word remains unuttered. Unless I love, His love cannot be expressed. With my thought God can reveal His thought. With my will He can show forth His will. What God has ordained is that all independent actions must be broken so that His Spirit may come forth through my spirit by using my will, mind and emotion.

In standing to give a message a brother may have a burden, but if he cannot find the thought, his burden will be of no avail. He is unable to use the burden of his spirit to save souls. In a person whose thoughts are confused, his burden has no outlet. It requires a broken outward man to release the inner burden. The spirit should not be blank and the outward man must have scars; otherwise, there will be blockage. If God had no need of the outward man, then whether the latter were broken or not would be of no concern. But God does require its breaking. He wants to break the outward man but not destroy it; for His work relies on the man being broken. Before brokenness occurs, the spirit and the outward man are opposite to each other in their relationship; but after brokenness, the inward and outward man are joined in one. The latter is under the control of the former.

When man was created he had spirit and soul (with a body as well). After man's fall due to sin, the inward and outward man do not seem to be opposite to each other; for the spirit still exists but there is in fact no inward man. The outward man has the power to break the inward spirit; thus the outward controls the inward. Today we are saved, but our condition has not yet been reversed. The outward man needs to be broken so that the inward may use the outward man. Just as in an unsaved person the outward man controls the inward spirit, so now in the saved the outward man should be broken and be put under the control of the inward man.

In serving, God must be given an outlet. In riding a bicycle, there are two possibilities: either the wheels run on the road when the road is flat and leveled, or the road runs the wheels when the road inclines downward. If the inward man is strong, it is like wheels running on the road; but if the outward man is strong, it will be like the road running the wheels. A bicycle is not like an airplane that can fly in the air. The measure of spiritual usefulness depends on how much the inward has control over the outward man. When the latter has its hands full of things, the Lord shows mercy in flattening the road by breaking the outward man in order to rid it of the things in hand so that the wheels may be in control of the road. Such "spiritual" flattening and riding are essential.

This breaking of the outward to release the spirit is not just a truth to be recognized and a theological doctrine to be understood. It is a work done in a person by God in order to make him a useful vessel. It is therefore absolutely necessary that the outward man be broken. Time and again, the hand of God is working. The eyes of the lowly donkey are brighter in such understanding than the eyes of the self-proclaimed prophet (see Num. 22.20ff.). Through the years God works with one definite direction and objective in mind, and that is, to break us. We ought to recognize His hand in breaking us. Today, we need to submit to God's arrangement. All our circumstances are arranged by Him. There is nothing accidental.

God's dealings follow a certain law. They are not governed by our prayers. Today the release of the inward man through the outward man is a law. It cannot be altered by prayer. If a hand is put in the fire, it results in pain, and the blood will clot, no matter how we pray (apart from a miracle). We should not be so foolish as to think that prayer alone can solve the problem. What we are saying today is that it is a law that the inward man is released through the outward man. Apart from this there can come no blessing. Unless the outward man is ground to powder, there can be no blessing. Self-choosing brings no blessing. God has decided to break the outward man, so obey this law. Do not just pray for blessing, for prayer will not change the law of God; nor will familiarity with this teaching alter the law. The way to spiritual usefulness lies in the breaking of the outward man. Without such breaking, our spiritual life is stifled. The responsibility is ours. Obeying God's law and submitting to His decision surpass tens, hundreds and thousands of prayers. This is the time to submit to His arrangement rather than to pray useless prayers in time of trouble. God chooses us to be His outlet. Many prayers for blessing hinder Him and prevent blessing. Submit, therefore, under the mighty hand of God.[*]

---

[*] Note: Message given on April 15, 1949.

Chapter 4

KNOW THE SPIRIT

How to Know People

A very essential part of the work for a worker who serves God is to know people. We must know the condition of the person before us. Where is his strength and how strong is he? Has he hidden something? What is his real state? What has he said and what is not uttered? Where lies the difference between uttered and unuttered words? What is his characteristic? Is his humility real or false? Is he stubborn or proud? The effectiveness of one's work depends on his knowledge of people's spiritual condition. The Holy Spirit makes known people's condition to our spirit, thus enabling us to speak the right word.

In the four Gospels the Lord is shown addressing the person before Him with the proper word each time. He spoke to the Samaritan woman about the "living water" (John 4.10); but He told Nicodemus about being "born anew" (John 3.3ff.). He would never tell the Samaritan woman about being "born anew," nor would He speak to Nicodemus about "living water." How appropriate His words were. To some, He called (cf. Matt. 22.14); while to those who would believe in Him, He said to "take up the cross" (Matt. 16.24, Mark 8.34, Luke 9.23). To others who ventured to follow Him, He asked them to "count the cost" (Luke 14.28, 33); and to still others who desired to postpone their coming after Him, He said to them to "leave the dead to bury their own dead" (Matt. 8.21-2, Luke 9.59-50). These differences are all due to the fact that the Lord knew each one of them. No matter even if He was being tempted, His words were always appropriate and effective (see Matt. 4.1-11, Luke 4.1-13). At first, we who begin to serve God follow the Lord at a distance. The Lord of Glory who performs glorious things is far ahead of us. We follow from afar, yet we follow on. We must learn how to know people little by little.

When souls are committed to the care of a young brother, he does not have the discerning wisdom, but has only one word that he especially likes. To whomever he meets, he gives the same word or teaching. It is like a physician who has only one prescription for all diseases. The young brother has yet to know the complexity of human beings. He cannot expect to use one spiritual word to heal all kinds of conditions. In such matters a sharp mind is as useless in touching people's spiritual state as is a dull mind.

The first thing a worker needs to learn is to find out the needs of the people. What people say may not be reliable. The one who is sick can only relate his symptom; the physician must give the diagnosis. When the sick speaks of his need, he may not be correct. Yet those who have studied physiology may find it comparatively easy to understand people's real condition as they synthesize the various symptoms. Do not coerce a patient to believe in a sickness he does not have. Only the subjective will insist on pressing his decision. It should not be done, for it will cause a big problem.

What we need is to learn before God how to diagnose a patient, finding out his true spiritual condition. If I know that I do not have the ability to help, then I should pray for him. If what is called for exceeds my power and my measure, I should not pretend that I am able to do anything. Sometimes I am able to help, in which case I should give my all; otherwise, I will learn how to pray. I should ask the Lord to give me grace and mercy for having fallen short in what I have learned.

Undoubtedly when there are problems in the body of Christ or among the fellow-workers, there is the need for other brothers and sisters to give assistance. Yet during such times, those who are strangers have no way to assist. The spiritual lives of many will be damaged if I insist on having them accept my subjective opinion without any objective help. If we would be of assistance to the children of God, we have the responsibility to learn to find out what are people's spiritual needs.

The Instrument of Knowing

A physician uses all kinds of instruments to help him diagnose. For taking a temperature he trusts not his own hand but puts his trust in a thermometer. He depends on instruments, not on himself. A servant of God has no instrument to help him diagnose people's spiritual state; yet God will so work in us that we ourselves become the thermometer, the x-ray, and so forth. Had not the thermometer been invented, the hand of the physician would have needed to be thoroughly trained and carefully protected. Since God wants *us* to be the diagnostic instrument, how diligently we must learn. The more thoroughly we are trained and the more drastically the cross works in our lives, the more useful we will be in helping others. He who preserves himself is not able to deal with others. A proud and narrow-minded person is unable to deal with people of his own kind.

In physical treatment the physician need never have been a patient. But both he who serves God and the one who asks for help begin from the same condition of need. Anyone who has not learned is incapable of leading people. We are the diagnostic instruments used by God; we therefore need to be accurate. A physician dare not use a defective thermometer. The instrument he uses must be accurate. Our responsibility in diagnosing people's spiritual situation is much greater than a physician's in the physical realm. The Spirit of God will not work independently; He works through the spirit of man.

People are helped partly through the discipline of the Holy Spirit and partly by the supply of the church — that is, by the ministry of God's word. If a minister of the word cannot discern the spiritual need of the people, then the supply of the church is missing. Whether a person is usable or not determines the measure of the supply of the church. God uses us to find out where the problem lies: in mind, in emotion, in opinion, or in the exercise of the spirit. If we learn wrongly, our diagnosis will be undependable. If we are not dependable, then the Spirit of God is blocked, and God's children lose the blessing. We are the meters used by God. How can we fail in recognizing people's condition? The beginning of our spiritual usefulness lies in being constantly adjusted, frequently corrected. The mercury in the thermometer must be refined to its purest state; otherwise its result will be inaccurate. Even the thermometer glass must have its standard, or else its speed in transmitting heat will be irregular. With a proper standard, the temperature will rise properly degree by degree. The instrument must be tested and retested until it is totally dependable. The usefulness of a meter lies in its accuracy. In case of inaccuracy, great mistakes will result. For us to be accurate, we need to go through strict dealings, for God wants to use us as thermometers to measure the various spiritual conditions of His people.

The Way of Learning

The way of learning is two-fold: one involves learning from the patients, the other, learning from ourselves. Let us begin with learning from the patients. Suppose a person walks in a dark night. As he hits a wall, the first member of his body wounded will be the nose. Accordingly, the condition of this projected member constitutes his specific condition. Similarly, in the spiritual realm, the impression given forth will invariably express the kind of person he is, whether his spirit is arrogant, hard, sorrowful, flippant or melancholic. Although the spirit itself is colorless, before the dividing of the outward and inward man, the latter is clothed with the former. As a result, the color of the outward man becomes the color of the inward man. In other words, before the breaking of the outward man, the outward man gives color to the person. But soon after the outward man is broken, the person's spirit is able to release

God's Spirit to people, thus giving forth the character of the Spirit of God. In order for our spirit to be clean and holy the outward man must be wounded and broken.

Upon the release of the spirit, any coloring of the outward man that is expressed by a person indicates his being unbroken in that point. It is here that people can touch such a condition. The spirit comes forth, as it were, riding on the back of the special condition of the outward man. Yet we must be warned, for our diagnosis will be impaired should we have the same condition. Those who have learned the lesson of the breaking of the outward man can touch the condition of people as to whether they have a haughty spirit, a darkened spirit, a heavy spirit, or a sorrowful spirit. It is then that we come to know their needs. The first secret of knowing people is to touch their spirit.

The condition of the spirit depends on the condition of the outward man. For the latter gives color to the inward man. People may not know that each time their projected point touches you, there lies their need for special dealing.

The second way of learning is through our being dealt with by God. The Spirit of God is in us. Each time He deals with us, His discipline gives us a lesson to learn. Once He disciplines us, it causes us to break a little. In whatever thing we are disciplined we are being broken in that particular thing. But for us to reach the point of usefulness, such discipline has to occur not just once, but sometimes several times, even many, many times. In whatever point we have been disciplined and broken, in that very point we are able to touch others. If we have not been broken in a certain area, in that very area we are unable to touch another's spirit; hence, we cannot help people in that area. This ability is so real that it cannot be imitated. For this reason we must undergo much brokenness in order to be more serviceable. Those who are broken more and pass through more have more to give.

Should one protect himself in a particular area he is deprived of being spiritually useful in that same area. In whatever thing he preserves himself, excuses himself or saves himself, he is rendered useless in making any spiritual contribution. Without that cutting away of the outward man, he lacks spiritual supply. He may live a comparatively easier life, but he will not experience more useful days for God. The underlying principle is that the measure of life-giving supply depends on the degree of being dealt with. A ten-year lesson can be learned in one year or a two-year lesson can require ten years to learn. Slowness in learning means delay in service. The way of service lies in the way of discipline. It is in the way of brokenness. The more there is of being dealt with, the keener will be the ability to know people. The more there is of being disciplined, the more readily one touches people.

Many have no spiritual discernment. They lack the power of distinguishing because they have learned too little. The Holy Spirit is once given, but the learning of man's spirit is lifelong. If the Lord has done something in our lives, the moment self raises its head in others, our spiritual sense recognizes it. Spiritual sense is gained gradually after many dealings. Much dealing gives more spiritual sense. For instance, we know that pride is a sin. Our teaching, thought and opinion may all condemn pride as sin, yet our spirit may not abhor pride. Yet once our pride has been seared, our spirit will react with abhorrence at the appearing of the spirit of pride in other people. Only those who have been sick and healed know what sickness is. It takes a lifetime to acquire this spiritual sense.

He who loves his soul life shall lose his soul life. The more one loses his soul life the more he learns. Never let anything go by without learning the lesson from it. The Lord leads us through fire in order to teach us lessons. The more the dealings, the more the service, the more the supply, and the more the ability to know people. As the dealings increase, so the service is broadened.

How to Deal Practically with People

Ordinarily, to touch people's spirit you must wait till they open their mouths. As one opens his mouth he utters what his heart is filled with. As he speaks, his spirit will come forth. Do not pay attention to what he says; rather, pay attention to his spirit. Then, knowing the spirit through the word, deal with the spirit. When the two disciples asked permission from the Lord to call fire down from heaven to consume the Samaritans the Lord rebuked them by saying to them that they did not know what kind of spirit they possessed (Lk. 9.54). As the words come out, the spirit follows suit. So, in listening to people, do not be entangled by the things said but try to touch their spirit. If the spirit is wrong, then all is wrong. If the spirit is right, he cannot be too wrong.

In the striving of the church, many spirits are wrong. Problems must be decided by the spirit. Never be drawn into the problem itself but stand on the ground of the spirit. Use your spirit to touch all sorts of spiritual situations. You can even touch the hidden spirit. Therefore, a worker must learn to use his spirit to know people, even as did Paul, who did not know Christ after the flesh (see 2 Cor. 5.16). This is a basic lesson for the worker.*

---

* Note: Message given on April 16, 1949.

Chapter 5

LIMITING GOD

Many are unconscious of the great difficulty that the outward man gives to God. Had they understood the true work of God they could not but confess that the outward man is indeed a tremendous hindrance. Today God suffers great limitation from the Church. He puts himself, as it were, in human bodies; therefore, these ones ought to be the fullness of God. Yet these people become His limitation. However, there is one man, even Jesus of Nazareth, who is an exception. Before the Word became flesh God was limitless, for with Him there is no boundary. After God became flesh He then was confined by the flesh. Yet the Lord Jesus did not limit God at all.

Today God commits himself to the Church. He entrusts all His works to the Church. Beginning from the time of Pentecost, God has not worked by himself alone. He today is in the Church just as in the former day He was in Christ. As He committed himself totally without limitation or reservation to Christ, so He confines himself to the Church today. The plight of the Church becomes the dilemma of God. In Christ God was never restricted, for the Son worked only after He had seen the Father so work. The Son would not speak out of himself nor would He judge by himself. He never testified out of His own self. He was the grain of wheat that died to release life to many grains. He neither hindered nor restricted God.

Today God chooses the Church to stand in the place of Jesus. He commits His limitlessness to the Church. The latter is where He speaks and where He manifests His power. Outside of the Church there is no work of God, for He dwells in the Church today. All the teachings in the Epistles of the New Testament teach us that God is in the Church. No Church, no work of God. In the Gospels God is shown to have been in one Man. In the Epistle to the Ephesians it says that God is only in the Church. He dwells not in organizations or institutions. May the Lord open our eyes to see this glorious fact. Had we heard and seen this we would prostrate ourselves at a distance, confessing: "O Lord, how greatly we have inhibited Your work!" Christ did not inhibit God in any way. Today God who dwells in the Church should be almighty and without limitation, such as we find in the Gospels. The limitation of the Church limits God. To limit the Church is to limit God.

When the children of Israel crucified Jesus, the apostle said they had crucified the Lord who gave life. When people persecute the Church, they persecute the Lord. The disability of the Church causes the limitation of God, for He has already committed himself to the Church. Simply put, our personal impediment hinders God. Our own hesitation becomes His limitation. The Lord says, "I am the way, and the truth, and the life" (John 14.6a). God comes forth by this way. We come to Him also by this way. Should He find no way in us, He is shut in by us.

Here we can see the importance of the discipline of the Holy Spirit and the dividing of the spirit and the soul. The outward man must be broken by God before He has a way out through us. What we are sharing now is more than a matter of personal experience; it is related to God's way in this age. Should man restrict God? Under our present condition He cannot freely release himself. Only after we accept brokenness will He be able to manifest himself in us.

May we realize that God's way is in and through us. May we provide Him the way of release. The Church is able to make this way available to God. Our outward man must be broken; otherwise, this issue of the way of God cannot be solved. How our human thoughts and feelings control us. How God is limited by us. May He give us grace to have our outward man broken.

In Reading the Bible

If we use our mind to read the Bible, the Bible we receive will be according to the kind of person we are. In using the mind to read the Bible, whether our mind is clever or confused, we fail to touch the spirit. For God to reveal himself through His written word, we need to touch it with the spirit. A remarkable thing about Bible reading is that unless our thoughts are objective, and our unharmonious thoughts are put away, our thought becomes a great hindrance to God, no matter how clever a person we may be. Our human thought has no way to enter into Bible thought.

There are two essential factors in Bible reading: our thought needs to enter into Bible thought, and our spirit must enter into Bible spirit. Our thought must enter into that of the writers who were inspired by God to write the Bible. In this way our thought and the thought of the inspired writer come to be in sync with each other. Our thought should enter into the other's thought. A subjective person or a clever person is unable to enter into the spiritual thoughts of the Bible writers. Oftentimes people read their own thoughts into the Scriptures. Their mental gears are moving, they expecting to get a little doctrine or a little teaching. Their heads dominate the reading of the Bible.

An unbroken mind seeks to establish its own system in the Bible. As a result, you cannot know the word of God. God wants to break your thought so that you no longer cling to your thought trend and system. Your entire way of thinking is thus broken; you let go of your own dominating thought. By this dealing you are enabled to touch the spirit of the Bible writer. (In preaching, some use their thought to quote the Bible, while others allow their thought to enter into the thought of the Holy Spirit and thus they have entered into the thought of the Bible. These two are in two totally different worlds.) The outward man must be broken before one can know the Bible. This is a fundamental principle for reading the Scriptures. Man's mind that has been poisoned by the serpent must be broken. For one to read the Bible correctly, his thought needs to enter into the thought of the Bible writer. This, however, is only the first step, though a most important step.

God's word is composed not just of thoughts as the writers of this world have thoughts. On the contrary, the Bible not only contains thoughts but also exhibits the spirit of the writers. This is where the Bible differs from all the other books in the world. The spirit of the Bible writers is exposed. In listening to the word of the prophet we realize there is spirit as well as thought in his word. The spirits of the majority of Bible writers are quite noticeable, such as those of David, Moses, John, Paul and others.

For this reason the second requirement in reading the Scriptures is that our own spirit must break forth to touch the spirit of the Bible writer. Suppose a true Christian mother has a naughty son who breaks the window of another's house and is severely beaten by the owner of that house. When the son comes home crying, the mother asks him why he cries. Did he break the other's glass intentionally or accidentally? The son acknowledges that he did it intentionally. So, the mother says to him, "I will also spank you." However, the spanking of the mother and the beating by another person are totally different in spirit. Only one who has the spirit of a mother knows how to discipline a child.

The spirit of Bible writing is not limited by time but is an eternal spirit. Our spirit today is able to touch the spirit of the Holy Spirit as of the time of the writing long ago; that is, to touch, for example, the spirit of Paul at his time. If our spirit fails to touch the spirit of the Bible writers, the words in the Scriptures are dead to us. Hence, on the one hand we need to touch the Bible thought with our thought, and on the other hand we need to allow our spirit to enter into the spirit of the Bible writers. Only after the outward man is broken can our thought be useful and our spirit be released. Our inability to do so hinders God's work. We do not give Him liberty to do what He desires. However, God wants to use us, and has enlisted us in His work. He wants us to know His word. He puts His word in our spirit so that we can use it to serve the church.

"But we will continue steadfastly in prayer, and in the ministry of the word" (Acts 6.4). Both the words "ministry" and "word" here are nouns. The apostles fulfill their ministry *with* the word. So, it is "the ministry of the word." God gives one or two words to man, and man uses this word or these words to serve people. Sometimes we have the word in our spirit — that is, we have the burden — but we are unable to discharge that burden with the word. The outward man does not have the suitable words with which to express the inner burden. Having failed to discharge the burden, we carry the original burden back home. All this is because the outward man has not been broken. There are not the living words by which to assist the inward man. Had there been the living words, the burden of the spirit would have been lightened. When the inward burden meets the insubordination of the outward man, God finds no way to express himself and the church is not blessed. The outward man is the greatest hindrance to Him. Only those who have been broken by God have the words to release the burden within. The shell of the outward man, especially its thoughts and feelings, must be broken, or else none can be a minister of God's word.

According to the Gospels, a woman who had had an issue of blood for twelve years came behind Jesus and touched the border of His garment, and immediately she was healed. Power had gone forth from Him (see Luke 8.43-48). Power came forth from the outermost of His body (the garment of Aaron represents the outermost of the body). Many brothers and sisters have life within them, yet their life is unable to launch out. The word within is blocked by the unbroken outward man.

Preaching the Gospel

Concerning this matter of preaching the gospel, many think people will believe if the doctrine is correct. Some even trust in their emotion to convert people. Thought and emotion are usable, but having them alone is not adequate. People are saved when our spirit is released in preaching the gospel. Only with the breaking of the outward man can the Spirit of the Lord be released from our spirit. Men such as D. L. Moody, Charles Stanley, Evan Roberts, Professor Moorehead, George Whitefield, Charles G. Finney and John Wesley have been raised up by God during the past two centuries.

In Scotland there was a man by the name of James M'Kendrick who wrote a book entitled *Seen and Heard*. He was a common laborer — a coal miner — and his English was not that great. Yet, his daily life touched others deeply. He did not have any special gift, nor was he a powerful man. But what was special in him was that his spirit was a broken spirit. When M'Kendrick was about eighteen years old, he was invited to preach. He wrote down an outline of his message, but through fear he forgot his outline. Upon standing to deliver his message, he bowed his head and prayed. He stood there weeping for half an hour; then, after saying a few words he came down from the pulpit. He thought to himself that the door that had been opened to him to minister God's word would henceforth be shut; he not knowing, however, that sixteen old and hardened sinners had been saved. Wherever he now went, people got saved. In fact, many were saved through him.[*]

When the hardness of the outward man is broken, it is not anger nor laughter (that is, levity) nor scolding but the spirit that comes forth to touch people. Do not surmise that such things as big gift, great power or eloquent speech can touch the audience. It is the spirit that moves the people. Many are wonderfully saved without knowing why. When the spirit rushes out, sinners get saved. The Spirit was able to be released because this simple Scottish laborer's spirit was a broken spirit. Unless we are broken we will be useless to God. Nowadays we need broken men to preach the gospel, for this is the current way of recovery. Gospel preaching must be recovered unto fruitfulness.

As soon as one is saved he should consecrate himself to God and forsake all to serve Him, just as people mentioned in the book of Acts did. As they went forth to preach, sinners had no way to hide themselves but surrendered to the Lord. The gospel of grace and the gospel of the kingdom were originally one, but later on they appear to be separated into grace first and then kingdom. Now, though, in the Lord's way of recovery, this

---

[*] For much more about M'Kendrick (b.1859), including lengthy excerpts quoted from his book see Watchman Nee, *The Spirit of the Gospel* (New York: Christian Fellowship Publishers, 1986), 4-15, 46-7. The full title of his book, first published sometime after 1927, is: *Seen and Heard during Forty-Six Years' Evangelistic Labours.* — *Translator*

gospel of grace and the gospel of the kingdom are reunited. Hereafter, people must be clearly saved, just as people were saved in the days of the apostles. In order for the gospel to be freely spread the gospelers must have a liberated spirit. From now on we need to pay a greater price. For the gospel to be recovered and the gospelers to be restored, it requires us to give our all. We are not able to go the way of recovery if we pay less.

Just as Jesus of Nazareth did not give God any restriction, the time has now come that the church should no longer limit God. Every disciplinary strike God gives is to bring the church to the place where she can manifest the move of God. For the past two thousand years the power of the gospel has been greatly reduced. This is because our consecration today lags far behind that of the early days. If we expect to be fully recovered, we must present ourselves more absolutely to God.[*]

---

[*] Note: Message given on April 18, 1949.

Chapter 6

THE DISCIPLINE OF THE HOLY SPIRIT

Not everyone has uncontrollable thoughts, nor do all have over-heated enthusiasm. For some their problem lies in overpowering thinking; for others, in uncontrollable feeling. But the problem with the will is quite common to all. Sometimes the difficulties in both emotion and mind actually originate with the will. It is easy for us to say with our mouth, "Not my will, but Thy will be done." Many who are not enlightened think it is easy to yield to God. People who speak so casually are far distant from light.

The root of the outward man is set in our will. Do not mistakenly think that consecration solves all problems. The truth is otherwise. Consecration is merely doing our part in putting ourselves unreservedly into God's hand. It cannot be inferred that from this God immediately makes us whole. True, without consecration there will not be a starting point on the spiritual path. With consecration we begin to walk in the right course. However, this does not mean that God has already done all His works in us. Consecration does not solve all the problems.

For a person to be serviceable to God there are two sides to be considered: consecration and the discipline of the Holy Spirit. Consecration plus the Spirit's discipline make a person a serviceable vessel of God. Consecration cannot be a substitute for the discipline of the Holy Spirit. Consecration is offering myself to God according to the light I have; whereas the discipline of the Holy Spirit is

God exercising lordship within us according to the light of the Holy Spirit. Consecration, since it is according to the light we have, is limited. Our condition may yet be darkness in the sight of God. Hence, our consecration cannot satisfy God's requirement nor fulfill His heart's desire.

Discipline, however, is according to the light of God. He knows our need, so He arranges our circumstances to break us down. This work far surpasses anything we could do of ourselves, for all the works of the Holy Spirit are done according to what God sees as to where our needs are. Therefore, the discipline of the Holy Spirit is thorough and complete. On the other hand, because we do not know what will happen, our choice is often wrong. There is no comparison in depth between consecration and discipline.

The discipline which the Holy Spirit has arranged far surpasses our thought. As a result, the children of God are frequently confused by such discipline. Many disciplinary acts seem to come suddenly. Our so-called light is so faint that it often is nothing but darkness. Discipline is what the Holy Spirit arranges for us according to the light of God. What really is "discipline"? God knows us well. Although we often think we know ourselves, actually we do not. So, from the time we accept the Lord He begins to arrange our circumstances to discipline us. The work of the Holy Spirit is sometimes positive and sometimes negative. The Lord dwells in us. What He gives us is Spirit which is life. This is positive for it builds up. When He enters us, we become a dual person. On the one hand, there is the Lord and the Spirit that God brings into us. On the other hand, there is our original person that is called the outward man. To build up the inward man is the work of the Holy Spirit. Yet in so doing, He must also do the negative work of arranging our circumstances in order to break down the outward man. Being born again is the positive work of the Holy Spirit; it is a building work. Discipline is His negative work; it is a breaking, weakening work. He sees the strength of the outward man, and so He deals with it because it poses a problem to the inward man.

This can be compared to wearing a narrow new shoe. The outward man gives the inward man a great deal of trouble. In the outward man we have an intense feeling, a wild thought and a strong will. We have a hard shell which imprisons our inward man. In the unbeliever the outward man has subdued the inward man. But in those who have believed the Lord for a number of years the Holy Spirit is breaking the outward man. The way God chooses to break it is not by strengthening the inward man to do the work of breaking the outward man. Rather, God chooses to deal with the latter with outside circumstances. The inward man is strengthened through the Holy Spirit, and the outward man is weakened by outside things. Due to the inadequacy of words, we call this "the discipline of the Holy Spirit." It does not refer to the inner control of the Holy Spirit but points to His arranging outside circumstances to rule over us, thereby causing us to reach His goal. He is pleased to employ outside things to deal with the outward man. It is not easy for the inward man to strike down the outward man. A person of feeling is affected by feeling. For the outward man can be hurt by outer things more than by any other way. What needs to be broken differs in every person. Even that worthless sparrow will not fall to the ground without the permission of the heavenly Father. All our hairs have been numbered; none will fall out without God's permission.

All the circumstances of the saints are arranged by the Lord. Everything is ordered by Him. Whatever happens to a Christian is prearranged. All our environments are God's ordering. Even our hairs have been numbered. Hairs are the most insignificant and tiniest things in our body. God points to this to show us how everything is under His arrangement. He alone knows how to break our outward man. Never consider anything which happens to us as accidental. All things which happen to us are God's way to build us up. He causes us to receive the discipline of the Holy Spirit. All our happenings are measured out to us by God. Do not ever assume that poor environment, bad turn of events, great difficulties and woeful things come from the work of man as if someone wants to hurt you or that your fate is doomed. Please remember, whatever God has done to us is to discipline us and is for our good. Where would we be today if He had not used these things to break down our outward man? This is God's method to keep us pure in His way. Please do not murmur, for insubjection and murmuring are altogether foolish. This is the best discipline we can ever have.

The discipline of the Holy Spirit is the ordering of our circumstances according to what God knows of us. The Holy Spirit commences this work on the day we are saved. He is free to work beginning from the day we consecrate ourselves to God. On those who are saved but not consecrated, the Holy Spirit also works, but He cannot freely work. So, He will wait till we have some light and our hearts are constrained to offer ourselves to God. Life or death, joy or pain: we put all in the Lord's hand. Such consecration gives the Holy Spirit freedom to work. After we have offered ourselves unconditionally to God, the Holy Spirit is able to work in us boldly without any reservation. All who walk in this way must pay attention to the work of the discipline of the Holy Spirit.

After a person is saved God never fails to give him grace. Each and every one has certain ways by which to receive grace — such as prayer, listening to preaching, assembling together, and reading the Bible. Day by day we live such lives of receiving grace. Daily we receive more grace. Yet even when we put all these ways of receiving grace together, they do not measure up to the discipline of the Holy Spirit. Under God's ordering there is no single way of receiving grace that is more important than the discipline of the Holy Spirit. This is because through it God breaks the outward man. The growth of many people still relies on prayer, listening to messages, and the half-an-hour Bible reading in the morning. They miss the principal way of receiving grace. The things which we encounter daily — in the hospital, in school, on the road and at home — offer us the most opportunities. Failure to see this creates the greatest loss, for we miss out on the best way of receiving grace.

Reading the Bible cannot substitute for the discipline of the Holy Spirit. Assembling together cannot replace it.

None of the other ways of receiving grace can be an alternative to it. No one can be a good Christian without learning to accept and to experience discipline. None may serve God without it. True, listening to messages may nourish us, prayer may awaken us, and reading the Bible may feed us. These may indeed refresh our spirit. But discipline is to purify us, it is a getting rid of mixture. The greatest profit comes from the arrangement of the Holy Spirit. If we are able to submit and not quarrel with God, the Holy Spirit will discipline us from all sides. God's hand will never draw back until we are freed from things such as field, house, herd and flock, clothing, and so forth. He will not overlook the smallest item. His purpose is completion. He will never withdraw His hand.

For some, God will arrange all kinds of people for them. When He uses people to deal with us, we begin to see our ugliness. Sometimes He will deal with our thought, be it confused, wild, clever or overly meticulous. He allows us to hit the wall and be defeated. After we have failed and received grace, we will then be afraid of our own thought as though fearing the fire. Some may be overly sensitive, some may be flippant in joy, some may be depressed to the point of laziness. The Lord will so deal with their emotions that they dare not be unduly joyful or sorrowful.

Some have a strong will and are self-confident. The apostle Paul received such grace that he dared not trust his flesh nor believe in himself. Our "self" must be brought to its end either by ourselves or by other people. Then we dare not have confidence in ourselves. After being dealt with again and again, after being defeated more and more, we are brought to the place where we will lower our head and dare not think or act out from ourselves. Sometimes, due to the lack of communication we may lack the supply of the word or the ordinary way of receiving grace. But the grace of discipline is not restricted by distance. We can always prostrate ourselves before the Lord. The grace of discipline surpasses all the supplies of the other means of grace. The discipline of the Holy Spirit is the greatest gift in life. It is not affected by our efforts, wisdom great or small, or gift more or less. God is not partial to anyone. The positive cannot substitute for the negative. The only way is to hand ourselves over unconditionally to Him. Then discipline will come upon us.

The cross is not a doctrine but a practice. God will allow us to practice it. Many things cannot be done through prayer but only by discipline. Bound when entering the fire, we shall have no smell of fire upon us upon our coming through the fiery trial (see Dan. 3.19-27). After being smitten many times, we naturally dare not be proud or careless anymore. Humility prompted by memory may not last for five minutes. Only after being smitten many times, perhaps twenty or even twenty-one times, will the memorized humility be gone and the natural pride fade away. Beatings alone can break down the outward man. No teaching, doctrine or memory can break it down. Beating is the only natural way for the breaking of the outward man. Hereafter, our will fears its own judgment as though fire. Such work is dependable and lasting. After the inward man is strengthened through grace and after the outward man which stands in the way of God's work is broken, then the inward and outward man become harmonious and united. In the beginning the outward man may tremble in fear and dare not join itself with the inward man. But this will be overcome later on.

Daily God disciplines us. Everything which happens to us is unto this end. The Lord must break our outward man. The enlightened will prostrate earlier, but even the foolish will slowly come around. There is no need to maintain it by memory. God has no need of our memory. He will so break us that even when we forget we shall still remain humble and dare not raise our head in pride. We will sense pain should we become proud. God wants us to depend on His grace, not on our ability to remember. How many times we resist, being foolish and proud, wanton and careless. We know that the work of God's hand is to break the outward man. Do not try to build before the outward man is broken, for it is futile. Eventually, we shall see how God does His work inside us.[*]

---

[*] Note: Message given on April 19, 1949.

Chapter 7

THE DIVIDING OF SOUL AND SPIRIT

The discipline of the Holy Spirit gradually breaks down our outward man. However, God wants to divide our spirit and soul as much as He wishes to break our natural man. Truly, it is most difficult to find a pure spirit. Many lack such a pure spirit. Their spirit is mixed and is not serviceable to God. The strength of service depends not on whether the measure of power is great or little; rather, it is determined by the purity of the spirit as to whether it is pure or mixed. Some people destroy much more than they build. On the one hand, they build with power; on the other hand, they destroy with a mixed spirit. How very often we see that such powerful men are mixed up with their "self." The more experience we have, the more we see these mixtures. For these outward things belong to the outward man. Those who know God treasure purity more than greatness and power.

If the outward man is not broken, one cannot expect a man's power to be pure. He will mix his self in it without feeling unclean or sinful. We know the gospel is the power of God. Yet, when one proclaims the gospel and mixes with it his jokes and flippancy, his listeners will touch mixture as well as power. Sometimes, even the zeal of proclaiming the gospel comes from man's delight. How much of our doing God's will is blended in with our pleasure. How much of our standing up for Him is supported by our strength. So, the work of God today is the ridding of such mixture as much as the breaking down of the outward man. The latter acts like an outer shell that inhibits the life of God; so He arranges outside circumstances to break down the outward man, to remove the hard shell. But where the outward man has mixed itself in with the spirit, the way of cleansing the mixture depends mainly on revelation. These two dealings are fundamentally different. One is the breaking of the outward man and is done through the discipline of the Holy Spirit. The other is the getting rid of the mixture and is done through the revelation of the Holy Spirit. Although distinct, these two things are nonetheless closely related. We need not only the breaking of the outward man, we also need the spirit to launch itself out clean and pure, without it being colored or tainted by mixture.

Oftentimes, when a brother is preaching, you may be able to touch God on the one hand and touch the preacher himself with his impurity on the other. The spirit is released but it comes out mixed with other things. If one is enlightened by the Holy Spirit, his outward man has been judged. But with the unenlightened, his outward man has not been judged; therefore, he is unaware of the mixture. The strong point of his outward man will inevitably come out with the spirit. No one can depend on memory in order to be spiritual, for memory is neither the salvation nor the rescue. As one opens his mouth, self will be exposed. If he keeps his mouth shut, the spirit inside is not easily revealed. But as soon as he opens his mouth, his spirit is manifested.

No matter how we pretend, it will not remain disguised. To be truly delivered we must start from within. Without receiving from God such basic dealing we try to be spiritual when we remember, but we become unspiritual when we forget. Mixture is a big problem in the lives of God's workers. It is as though there were two kinds of water gushing out of the same fountain. Many, as they stand up to speak, give the audience a mixed and impure impression. A minister of God's word should ask God to break the outward man and to divide the outward man from the inward man. In order for one to be used by God his spirit must be released in purity. The impurity of one who lives carelessly will sooner or later be manifested in his ministry. The name of the Lord as well as the name of the Church will suffer greatly if there is mixture in our spirit.

The discipline of the Holy Spirit may precede revelation, or vice versa. They may also differ in order in preaching. However, although the order in which they occur is uncertain, in experience they are inseparable. Some receive discipline before revelation, others receive revelation ahead of discipline. Although in experience discipline occurs more frequently than revelation, the result of discipline peaks in revelation. Spirit and soul must be divided. The outward and inward man must be separated. The outward man needs to be broken so that the spirit can be released in pureness.

How does the revelation of the Holy Spirit break the outward man? Hebrews 4.12-13 says: "the word of God is living, and active, and sharper than any two-edged sword, and piercing even to the dividing of soul and spirit, of both joints and marrow, and quick to discern the thoughts and intents of the heart. And there is no creature that is not manifest in his sight: but all things are naked and laid open before the eyes of him with whom we have to do." Now in Young's Literal Translation of the Holy Bible, both "word" in verse 12 and "to do" in verse 13 are translated out of the original with the same word "reckoning." Reckoning is "the settlement of a bill or account." It can also be considered as "judgment." So verse 13 should be literally translated as: "And there is not a created thing not manifest before Him, but all things are naked, and open to His eyes – with whom is our reckoning." For this reckoning God uses His living word. When His word is really seen by man, it is truly living.

Unfortunately, people usually touch the letter instead of the living word of God. His word is living: this points to its inward reality. His word is active, for it is effective in us. His word is piercing, sharper than a two-edged sword. It pierces through what a two-edged sword cannot penetrate. Just as the sharp sword pierces through the bones and marrow, so the word of God divides the soul and the spirit. Physiologically speaking, man's deepest place in body is bones and marrow, yet the sharp sword of God can pierce and divide. Bones are to be horizontally divided while marrow is to be vertically cleaved; accordingly, the inward and the outward are divided. Thus is it with the body. Yet there is something more difficult than the piercing to the dividing of bones and marrow, which is the piercing to the dividing of soul and spirit. However, the word of God is well able to pierce and divide man's spirit and soul.

Piercing and Dividing

What is meant by the dividing of spirit and soul? This is explained by the following words: "quick to discern the thoughts and intents of the heart." When the word of God comes, it acts like a sharp two-edged sword that pierces and divides bones and marrow. The word of God is able to divide spirit and soul. How frequently we use such words as the outward man, the soulish, the carnal, the natural, and the self. We use these expressions lightly because we have not the light. We read about them and we talk about them. But when light comes to us with its overpowering brilliancy, it is sharper than any two-edged sword and exposes the very depth of our "self." Indeed, we often mention the word "self" carelessly as if it were common and cheap. We jokingly say this or that thing is fleshly, hated by God. Yet when light comes from above, we are smitten to the ground. For the dividing of spirit and soul is not just a matter of mental knowledge. It is God's word that is quick to discern the thoughts and the intents of the heart. It manifests how fleshly are our thoughts and intents—that both what we think about and what we desire after are fleshly.

There are two kinds of sinners. One kind is the knowledgeable sinners. They have heard that all have sinned. The preachers have presented this clearly and logically. And they themselves say that they are sinners. However, they say this without conviction. The other kind of sinners are those who are being enlightened by the same words. Instead of jokingly saying they are sinners, they prostrate themselves on the ground, confessing they are sinners. Since these are convicted by the light of the word, they fall to the ground and get saved. It is the light that manifests to them that they are sinners. In like manner, this matter of the outward man is most serious. The natural man must be broken in order that instead of using what one has heard as a subject of conversation, he is so enlightened that he can only cry out: "O Lord! Today I know this is the man whom You want to break down." As soon as light shines upon you, you immediately fall down.

What is meant by the revelation of the Holy Spirit? In many things which you do daily, even as you say that you love the Lord, when the light shines upon you, you see that your loving the Lord is actually your loving yourself. It is light, not teaching, which divides. Suddenly I see that what I had considered to be a lifetime of loving the Lord is nothing but the love of self, and that my zeal is all natural, not spiritual. Under the light, I see that even my preaching the gospel to sinners is motivated by my active nature as a person who likes to speak, to run and to be active. Now the light has manifested my thoughts and intents. I know all is actually out of myself. As soon as I see the light I cannot but fall down. The reason people fall down before the Lord is because they begin to see that what they consider to be of the Lord proves to be out from self. How many works have men done for the Lord, they thinking they are ordered by the Lord when they have actually been done by themselves. How many preaching services have been undertaken as though from the Lord, yet actually they have come from the preachers themselves. When the light shines, the spirit and the soul are divided. They are no longer joined together. What is natural is separated from what is grace. What is self is severed from what is God's.

How can we throw off the outward man? Some people still live by it after following the Lord for twenty years. They still flippantly talk about the natural and the fleshly. There does not seem to be any salvation. Yet salvation comes suddenly one day when light shines. Then, all these activities — such as talking about the natural in the natural man and about the fleshly in the flesh — are exposed. Under enlightenment, they see that all these things had come from their outward man. Through seeing the real intent and strength of the heart, they are delivered from the outward man. Such deliverance by dividing comes neither through resistance nor by coercion. Oftentimes, even the confession of sins is unclean. The tears shed for sins need the cleansing of the blood. None knows his own heart. One can see his real self only under the light. How we seek to build up ourselves! Light will deal with *us* — with our *very* selves — just as it deals with our sins.

How Do We Receive Revelation?

What is the criterion for seeing? All things are naked and laid open before the eyes of the Lord. God is the standard of light. Adam clothed himself with fig leaves, surmising he was covered. But God saw him as being still naked. No creature can hide himself from God. There is no covering whatsoever. All coverings are made to cover oneself, but they cannot conceal anything from God. They may hide us from seeing ourselves, but all things are naked before Him. For the Lord is all-seeing. Revelation means a being caused to know myself just as He knows me. The Lord opens my eyes to see the hidden intent and deep thought of my heart, to know my true condition before Him. I begin to see what He sees. Henceforth all is naked and open.

Some people live under the revelation of God, whereas others live outside of His revelation. The difference is that the enlightened will fall down under the light; their pride is gone. The dividing of spirit and soul comes through the revelation of God in showing us the thoughts and intents of our heart as He sees them. No one in this world knows his own heart. To "discern" is to "divide." When the thoughts of the heart are discerned, the intents of the heart are divided. In recognizing the flesh, the spirit is divided from the soul. So, the basic need is light.

Sooner or later light will come upon us. Under such light we come to "reckoning." The Lord is our reckoning. He is our judgment. In His light we begin to know ourselves. Under His enlightenment we see our fault. How we deceive our selves as well as our brethren in the church. All flesh is exposed under the light. We come to know ourselves. We realize how our service comes from self-love. Henceforth, we begin to differentiate what is of the soul and what is of the spirit. Those who are in the light and who have been judged or reckoned will later be able to deny whatever comes from self. But for those who have not been judged by the light, there is no way for them to discern and to deny.

After being judged or reckoned, you recognize what is from you yourself. Whenever it starts to rise up, it is judged. Before enlightenment, what you know is but knowledge and teaching. There is no salvation. It is dangerous to joke about oneself. Only after being enlightened are the spirit and the soul divided. This inner understanding is the dividing of spirit and soul. What the Lord must do in us is to shine in us with an overpowering light. When this takes place — and whether I am working or praying or I am with other brothers or alone by myself — I receive from God a matchless light that causes me to realize how much comes from myself and how little comes from God. Nay, probably nothing comes from God; everything seems to come from myself. It is I who am active, busily working in preaching and saving souls. How big is self, but how little is the Lord. On the other hand, as the light manifests me, the hidden "I" is now exposed. The things I did not sense in my thoughts and intents are now totally revealed.

Although outwardly all is being done in the name of the Lord, actually everything comes out of me myself. But with my having received the light, things are naturally manifested. Whenever the same thing happens for the second time, regardless whether it is principle or speech, its inward intent is immediately detected and thereby judged and rejected. Words spoken before being judged or reckoned are all of no avail. Therefore, we must live continuously before the Lord so that our spirit will be released in purity. Then will the Lord have no hindrance in using us; for whenever self raises its head, His light will immediately deal with it.

The dividing of spirit and soul depends on light. Light manifests the activity of the outward man, and at the same time it kills the soulish activity — whether it is stubbornness or an over-heated emotion. It is not the listening to messages that brings wisdom: it is light that works in people. To be enlightened is to see what God has seen. For He has seen what we have never seen—the intents of our heart. Then having seen it, we must deal with it. The word of God bears fruit. Seeing and fruit-bearing are one. As God sends out light the thing is done. His light is like the ultraviolet rays which kill germs. Being exposed to light, the fleshly activity of man will fall and be slain. Light withers the flesh, and thus seeing is fruit-bearing. The word of God is living and fruitful. Seeing light is gain; not seeing is loss. Enlightenment and discipline break us.[*]

---

[*] Note: Message given on April 20, 1949.

Chapter 8

THE LIGHT THAT KILLS

The two measures the Lord uses in enabling the use of the spirit are: (1) the discipline of the Holy Spirit to strike at the outward man, which happens under grace; and (2) the revelation He gives to break the outward man and cause the dividing of soul and spirit. We truly should put ourselves in the Lord's hand, absolutely and unreservedly giving ourselves to Him, willing both to be smitten under light and to be broken down in His arranged circumstances. In the lives of the saints more days and time are spent in having the outward man broken. Indeed, there is nothing in life that costs the Lord more time in doing His work. May we not waste the working of God nor delay the way of the Church. Let us give ourselves unreservedly to the hand of God, letting Him complete the work He deems necessary in us.

What is the condition of a broken person? What proceeds from us? The issue lies not in what we say or what we do but rests on what comes out of us. What is it that really issues forth from us? This one issue surpasses all which we may say or do. If we pay attention only to what we say or do, while what really issues out of us is altogether something different, we are not able to help people, for it is mixed and unclean. It holds back God's blessing.

It is our strongest point that impresses people. In case our mind is the strongest point of our life, then people will be touched by our wild or clever thoughts; or if emotion is our strongest point, people will be impressed by our over-heated or excessively cold emotion. It is what comes out of self which touches people. We can control our words and deeds, but we have no control over our strong point. Whatever that may be, it launches forth. There is no way of restraint.

It is a common saying, "I have a good or bad impression of him." Where does impression come from? It comes not from words and deeds. Rather, it is something other than words and deeds which impresses us and forms our judgment. What makes my impression is the "something other" in that person, with or without words and deeds. When you encounter this something other, you get the impression. Spiritual supply comes mostly from this something other rather than from words and deeds. It is that impression which either edifies or destroys. So, what goes out of the person is extremely important. Alas, in this we are totally helpless, for the impression we give will correspond without fail to our strongest point.

In 2 Kings chapter 4, there is the story of the woman of Shunem and Elisha. The woman constrained Elisha to eat bread, and so whenever the prophet passed by, he turned in and ate bread. And the woman said to her husband, "Behold now, I perceive that this is a holy man of God, that passeth by us continually" (v.9). The comment of D.M. Panton was: "Elisha while eating gave people the impression that he is a holy man of God." When Elisha was in Shunem, he neither preached nor performed miracles. He called no disciple, he was simply passing through Shunem; and yet in eating, he left such an impression to others. It is your strong point which is usually released from you and impresses others.

"Impression" is not created by words or deeds. It is conveyed according to your strong point. Whatever your strength is, you are released through it. Yet the "impression" the church needs is the release of the spirit. This release of the spirit is what God requires as well as what people need. But the spirit cannot be released unless the outward man is first broken. Lay a stone and a cloth together on the sand. The different qualities between the two are quite evident. We know what each's strength is. Just so, the strength of the outward man far exceeds our understanding. It must be broken.

Once a man spoke on the subject of the "Holy Spirit." Although his mouth was full of speech about the Holy Spirit, his body language was full of self. The word given was about the Holy Spirit, but the impression he left with people was self. Learn not how to preach and how to expound but learn to know what proceeds out of you. Never leave the impression that all is self. The issue lies not in preaching; it rests on what impression you give to people. Today God is not looking for our advancement in doctrine; rather, He wants to deal with our total being in order that we may render spiritual help to others. The unspiritual person cannot give spiritual impression but exhibits self instead. How pitiful this is.

God arranges our circumstances to chip away at our strong point, and He will not stop working till it is done. It is through the discipline of the Holy Spirit that this is accomplished in us. Ordinarily, in listening to the word of life, we first receive the teaching and after a while the Holy Spirit will lead us into the truth. Yet the discipline of the Holy Spirit is the process by which He works in us. It may take ten times of dealing before it chips away at self even a little. The understanding of what we hear comes faster than submission to discipline. The Lord, however, will eventually bring you to submission. He will continue to work till you confess: "O Lord! I dare not be obstinate nor proud nor have self-love." Such a lesson of discipline is learned slowly. The Lord may have worked ten times before we realize what is going on. Nevertheless, He will work on till He succeeds in bringing us to see and to attain.

The discipline of the Holy Spirit is not the preaching about the Holy Spirit. It is both a tearing down and a building up; and both are done simultaneously. It is seeing the teaching and receiving the edification. It is seeing the purpose of what the Lord has tried to deal with in the past years. Thank the Lord, that that particular point in you has been dealt with. Now you enjoy the fruit of discipline.

The Holy Spirit uses both discipline and enlightenment to deal with the outward man. Sometimes these two come simultaneously; at other times they come one after the other. God's work may come by revelation, or the Holy Spirit may use discipline alone to do the job. Flesh may hide only in darkness. It can be likened to bacteria which grows in darkness. The reason for the continued existence of the flesh is because we are ignorant of its presence. The flesh is not afraid of man's light; it is afraid of the light of God.

During the time of the richness of the church in having plenty of prophetic messages, light will come forth and people will begin to see that pride really abides in them and to see that it is hateful and unclean. The pride we see in the light of revelation is so ugly and dirty that it is altogether different from what we may have confessed before. We might have said we were proud, not knowing that this very acknowledgment was itself pride. Light places us in a different position. We begin to see ourselves many times more hateful than what we had confessed before. What is of the flesh and of the natural is now being withered. The marvelous thing is that what is seen in the light is also what is killed by the light. For killing and seeing are not two different things. It is not a matter of something of the self-life being killed after we have seen it for many years. No, the very moment we see the light, our self-life is finished.

The work of the Holy Spirit, whether it be discipline or revelation, is one. Under discipline and under revelation, people are being dealt with. Revelation not only causes people to see, it also kills what is seen. Even the pride of the proudest can be killed within a few hours. Revelation is the way the Lord ordains for us. Revelation is the way God works and it is the work of God. Revelation is light, and revelation kills. Whatever is hateful is condemned to death. The light that slays is the greatest of the experiences of the saints.

When Paul saw the light, he did not say, "All right," and then got off his horse to listen. The clearest in mind will immediately fall from the horse. Light causes one to fall. It finishes you. The human brain plays no part in it; otherwise, it would be two steps instead of one step. As the light strikes, one immediately falls. And thus, there is but one step. As God enlightens, I am finished. I cannot say I will change tomorrow. That would be the sense of the brain. But when light comes, the real condition is seen. Its uncleanness and hatefulness are exposed, and as a result it is withered. After being enlightened, the proud person dares not be proud again, for he senses the hatefulness and shamefulness of pride.

Be aware that it is at the moment the light comes that we see and fall down in prostration, not at the time of prayer and inquiry. Do not change the date of God speaking to the date of prayer. We are saved by receiving the light, not by praying for light. The principle of God's salvation remains the same regardless the timing of our experience.

As we prostrate ourselves before the Lord He gives us sufficient light to see how unclean we are. We see how many are the things we did in the name of the Lord, for the Lord, and as expressions of our love to the Lord; yet they were done out of the basest of motives under the guise of noble thoughts. Man's self will penetrate every loophole, even to the extent of robbing the glory of God. In our hearts there exist the basest and dirtiest intents and thoughts. It is the revelation of God that exposes and makes naked everything in us.

God knows us well, though we never know ourselves. But when His light shines upon us, it reveals all the thoughts and intents of our hearts and lays them all bare before our eyes. At that instant we are truly finished. We regret, are ashamed, and abhor ourselves. Thus is the "self" severely wounded. For how many years have we been blind, thinking well of ourselves. Now, though, we begin to see our ugliness and our pretension. We are so ashamed of ourselves that the mere recollection of our boasting gives us double shame. Under such a condition we repent at the feet of the Lord.

When Adam saw his nakedness he immediately felt ashamed, for nakedness and shamefulness go together. Things which could not be shaken off in a period of many years fall away as we bow our heads in shame. We need to see, we need enlightenment, before our strong point will wither, and before our outer shell (that which garrisons ourselves, considering ourselves as stronger than others) is set aside. The discipline of the Holy Spirit is one thing, and His enlightenment another. Discipline works slowly. It takes years and many occasions, and may not depend on the ministry of the word. But the revelation of the Holy Spirit is quite fast. It may come in a few days or a few minutes.

Oftentimes revelation comes through the supply of God's word. If the church is healthy, the words are rich and revelations are abundant. Yet even in the absence of much revelation, discipline will not be lessened. In spite of the lack of the supply of God's word, no one should preserve his outer shell, for the discipline of the Holy Spirit is still there. Many miss the supply of God's word because of the weakness of the church, but many lose the effect of the discipline due to their own foolishness. Many times

discipline yields no fruit; numerous times of chastisement
produce no understanding of God's will. This is not due to
any lack of discipline through the years; sadly, it is because
people fail to recognize the hand of God. In Psalm 39.9 it
says: "I was dumb, I opened not my mouth; because thou
didst it." How frequently we think it is our relatives,
friends and colleagues who give us troubles. We must
learn to see that it is God who is dealing with us. For many
years the Lord has tried to discipline us, but we always
blame other people, question our circumstances, and
wonder about our fate and happenings.

Let us understand that everything is measured out to us
by God. How long or short, how big or small, how heavy
or light, and where it will end up — all has been measured
out by Him. The Lord causes something to happen to us in
order to deal with and break down the thing within us
which is different from Him, so that we may understand
His way in us. We should ask for God's mercy to show us
the purpose of His past discipline. Also, in those days
when God begins to speak to us, let us ask Him to
enlighten us and expose us more with His words. Thus will
our outward man be broken. What proceeds from us will
no longer be our strength but will be our spirit touching the
spirit of others — a broken spirit that no longer is tainted
by self. The impression the spirit creates depends on the
outward man. If the latter is broken, its meekness is the
meekness of a broken spirit; for the spirit is released with
the changed condition of the outward man. If each time the
spirit launches forth it is done so with such broken

condition, the church will receive surpassing blessing, for whoever touches the spirit touches God.

The former [that is, the nineteenth] century was the century of truth recovered. Now let us ask the Lord for grace that the years and days ahead will be times of the change of man. Just as truth must be recovered, so must man be restored. God seems to be moving along the same path both in England and in China: not just that teaching be correct, but that teachers be right. God will meet the needs of many people through the release of our spirit. Nothing needs thorough dealing more than the self. We should ask the Lord, "What impression do I give to people? What do they touch — is it man or the Lord that is touching their spirit?" Nothing can substitute the spirit. Today the Lord pays less attention to your doctrine, teaching or message. He cares more about the impression you leave with others. What is it that comes out of you? In case the spirit is not rightly released, all activities are vanity of vanities.

The Lord notices what comes out of you much more than what proceeds from your mouth. Each time people contact you, they touch your strong point. A "something other" came out of the Lord; a "something other" came out of the apostles. What comes out from us? Is it the outward man, or God himself? The two disciples asked the Lord, "Lord, wilt thou that we bid fire to come down from heaven, and consume them?" And the Lord answered, "Ye know not what manner of spirit ye are of" (Luke 9.54-55 margin). What color does the spirit carry when it is released? What kind of spirit is being conveyed? Things of the outward man such as pride, uncleanness, self-love, and so forth? May we have the eyesight to see that there is a new way in the spiritual world. May the Lord break our outward man every day so that the spirit has a way to be released without it being mixed with the unrighteous outward man. May God deal drastically with this man of mine.*

* Note: Message given on April 21, 1949.

Chapter 9

A CONTRITE SPIRIT

How does God break down the outward man? Such breaking differs in different people. There are various kinds of arrangement and discipline. For some, what needs to be broken is self-love; for others, it is pride; and for still others, it may be cleverness. Yet in each and every one God will deal with what his strong point is and cause him to fail again and again in that particular area till he learns not to trust in his strength, till he reaches the place where he acknowledges that "I live not by man's wisdom but by God's grace."

It is recorded in Genesis, "Is anything too hard for Jehovah?" (18.14) There is nothing too hard for the Lord, nothing whatsoever. Never will He lower His head and acknowledge, "There is nothing I can do." With such a nearly impossible case, the Lord will cause him to be beaten and defeated each and every time. True, the way of the Holy Spirit differs according to each case. With some the Lord will strike without let-up, while with others He will strike and loose or relax in turn. Nonetheless, all whom the Lord loves, He will chastise (see Heb. 12.5ff.; cf. Prov. 3.11-12). Though the part being stricken may differ, the success is the same. Whatever may be the point of striking, that which is wounded is the "self."

The end result of each dealing is to weaken "self." Some people receive special dealing on emotion; while some others, on thought. Yet they all result in the breaking of the will; for we all are strong in this area. What maintains that strong will is emotion or cleverness. So, although what the Holy Spirit seeks to break and wound may seem to differ, eventually what has been dealt with is self. Our will may be dealt with by revelation or by discipline till it is softer. Meekness is a characteristic of being broken.

The reason why we are so strong is because we have many things which support us. These are like pillars that support a house. Tear down the pillars and the house will fall. Outward appearance may differ, but the strength of what is within is the same. Do not be deceived by a soft voice, thinking that such a voice represents a meek person. Strength lies not in voice but in character. He who is soft-voiced can be as stubborn as he who is loud-voiced and quick-tempered. After the Lord has taken away our supports one by one and after He has dealt with us many times and over several years, we dare not repeat our former way lest we again be hurt.

Thus, a person turns soft and tender. He is unable to be hardened as before lest he sin against the Lord. He dare not be loose, neither will he press for his own opinion or make his own move. Such "dare not" or "godliness" enables one to be contrite and broken. As there is more dealing, there will be increase in tenderness. So, this "contrite" spirit is the sign of brokenness. When you meet a person, you may realize he has gift but his person is still unbroken. This, indeed, is a pity. But when you encounter one who has been stricken and is broken, you touch a gentleness there.

It is as if he is saying: "I dare not be proud and careless." So, this is godliness, this is contrition.

There are many symbols used for the Holy Spirit in the Bible. He is as "fire," speaking of His power. He is like "water," signifying His cleanness. Or He is symbolized by a "dove," referring to His gentleness — in other words, the nature of the Holy Spirit is dove-like, not eagle-like. He is gentle, peaceful, restful and tender without any hardness. God will so work till His character is established in us. There will be more dove character built in us. Such tenderness that comes from godliness is the sign of being broken by the Holy Spirit. A softened person is easy to deal with. He is easy to be talked to and easily entreated. He is quick to confess sins, and weeps easily. He is prone to acknowledge his fault and ready to accept the ideas of others. He is teachable and open to the cry of other people. In other words, he is tender before God.

Indeed, after a person's emotion, thought and will are broken, he easily confesses and weeps because his shell has been broken. He is open to be taught and therefore he will be edified. A broken person can easily release his spirit, and can likewise easily allow the spirit of other brothers and sisters to touch him. In this condition, as soon as any spirit stirs, you immediately sense it. Your perception is so sharp that immediately you know what is happening, thus keeping you from doing anything wrong. Even in prayer, you can sense the feeling of the other person. How often, in spite of your sensing in the spirit that something is wrong, people continue praying. This is because their outer shell has not been broken. Sometimes during their prayer you feel like asking God to stop them, yet they still go on praying because they are insensitive. They are unable to react to how the spirit of another feels. On the other hand, brokenness both releases one's own spirit and also goes on to touch the spirit of others. Hence, he will not do anything that hurts the spirit of others nor will he tread on people's feelings. He will not be a person void of sense.

Only after the outward man is broken may one possess body or church consciousness. Before the outward man is broken there is no way to recognize the working of the body of Christ. It will be like having a mechanical hand that is void of any sensation. How many are void of inner sensitivity towards the body of the Lord. Yet, with the breaking of the outward man you are enabled to touch the conscience of the church, thereby having church consciousness. Your spirit is open and can be touched by the church. The spirit of the church is now in fellowship with your spirit. If my outward man is broken, as soon as anything is wrong, I will automatically sense it. If I am wrong, I will change at once, even before people open their mouths to correct me. Such, then, is a basic need for body life.

The consciousness of the body does not come by consultation; it comes from a contrite feeling. Such feeling expresses the sense of the body as well as reveals the mind of Christ the Head. The mind of the Head is manifested through the emotions of the body. Whatever the spirit rejects, you ought not interfere with. All this begins with the breaking of the outward man. Then our spirit will be changed into a communing spirit by which it can supply as well as receive the supply of the spirit of all the members of the body. Wherever they go, they may be helped by the smallest brethren.

Suppose that in a meeting there is a brother whose outward man has not been broken. He is, however, very intelligent. This brother cannot easily be helped in the meeting unless he meets another who is equally intelligent or even more intelligent than he. Were he to undergo many dealings with the result that he is now broken in mind, he would then realize how vain is his thought. His mind is broken under discipline, and he turns childlike, easy to be taught because he now has a contrite spirit. And let us say that sometime later a young man stands up to speak whose diction is poor and whose teaching may not be correct; yet the spirit of that more intelligent brother who now has a contrite spirit is being touched. Therein is the work of the Lord. Indeed, even an elderly brother who has been broken through discipline can testify that his spirit is revived and that he is being edified.

Regardless how young a brother is, he has the Holy Spirit. With a contrite and broken spirit, he can be helped whenever the spirit of another is released. And thus will he be able to receive help from the whole assembly. As soon as the spirit moves, he is edified. The opposite is also true with an unbroken person who fails to get any help while the spirit is moving. What builds up is not the increase of teaching, thought and idea; rather, it lies in the contact of my spirit with God's Spirit. Wherever I am, I am quickened as I touch the Spirit of God in another's spirit.

For our spirit is like a mirror. Each time it is enlightened, it is as if it is being touched and brightened. The contact of spirit with spirit gives light. It is therefore incorrect to look to accurate exposition and good teaching as the means for being built up spiritually. Regardless whether a meeting is good or bad, what builds up people is a touch of the Holy Spirit. Regardless the kind of light bulb, as long as the wire conducts electricity there will be light.

A person with an open spirit may easily be helped. How very difficult it is for many to receive help. In spite of much effort, there is little result. Yet, should their outward man be broken they will be open to the help of the whole assembly. With the release of the spirit they can be helped, and they also can help others. Here are two kinds of Christianity: one kind is characterized by helping the outward man with teaching, thought, truth and doctrine; the other kind is characterized by a touching of the inner spirit. Thank God, He touches my inward man and revives my spirit. This is true Christianity.

Doctrine is stored in our brain. It is not true edification. The real issue lies in the spirit. When the spirit of the one who preaches is released, my spirit is being washed. He may preach the same doctrine for the second time, but if his spirit is again released, I will be washed once more. Otherwise, it will be like watching a play in whose second performance I will lose my interest. Nonetheless, if the spirit is still able to be released even when one speaks on the same doctrine for the third time, my spirit will continue to be awakened and to be washed by the living water. The preacher's spirit will be tender and will touch my spirit. So, it is the spirit that edifies spirit. Even all truths are dead without the spirit.

Hence, a contrite and broken spirit is extremely important. Only a broken person knows how to edify people best. At the same time as he helps others he himself is also being edified. He is able to receive the supply of the entire assembly. All the members of the body seem to be able to give him supply. He becomes the biggest receiver under all sorts of situations. He obtains help from all the members. He becomes a vessel that is being benefited by everyone. The riches of the Head are the riches of the body, and the riches of the body become my richness. How vastly different is this from mere mental doctrine. Pay special attention to how people are helped. The measure of help people receive from you is the proof of your brokenness. On the other hand, your inability to help others proves the hardness of your shell. The same is true with regard to your difficulty in receiving help. The Lord uses all kinds of means to break us that we might be greatly helped. The more broken, the more help we receive.

In Shanghai many will listen only to sister Ruth Lee and sister Peace Wang[*]. Such a symptom shows that their shells are not broken. Why is it that the spirit of other brothers and sisters has gone unheard, and that we are untouched? If our outward man is broken, we will be touched and awakened each time the spirit is released — no matter from whom. The breaking of our outward man

---

[*] These were prominent fellow workers of Watchman Nee — *Translator*

determines whether we can be edified. This, therefore, is a foundational requirement of service.

I will myself confess that I receive more help from brothers and sisters who are spiritually behind me than from those who are ahead of me. How often I receive light and am refreshed by them. Do not despise the young people, even the youngest, for their help to you comes from the spirit. Seek to be edified in the spirit, seek to touch the spirit everywhere. Even a few words spoken in the spirit from God will be of help. Those who are able to release the spirit shall see the work of the Holy Spirit. "Brokenness" is a basic work of God. He must do this work, and then we will begin to know what fellowship is.

Fellowship is not the flow of thought to thought, nor is it the exchange of idea with idea. It is the touch and flow together of spirit with spirit. Only after the outward man is broken by the mercy of the Lord may we begin to understand the communion of the Holy Spirit. All supply and fellowship are in the spirit, not in doctrine. Frequently the so-called united prayer is but the prayer of the same brain. The fact remains that true oneness comes from the fellowship in the spirit. All who are born again and have life may have this fellowship in the spirit. When you allow God to break your outward man, then your spirit is able to be opened to accept the spirit of all your brothers and sisters. This is truly touching the body of Christ. It will be as is said in Psalm 42.7: "Deep calleth unto deep." There is the fellowship and response of deep with deep. In my deep I can touch the deep of the church.

Such brokenness comes from the work of the Holy Spirit. Man cannot do anything. All man's efforts are useless. It is not a matter of trying not to trust in self, not to love self, or not to care for self. No one can substitute the work of the Holy Spirit. If we attempt to imitate, we are actually adding more hardship to God. Meekness is the effect of the work of the Holy Spirit. Whatever is done in us comes not from our labor but comes exclusively from the discipline of the Holy Spirit. The Holy Spirit alone knows our needs and He arranges circumstances to break us. Our responsibility is to ask the Lord to be merciful to us in giving us light, causing us to realize God's hand and to submit ourselves without resistance to the Lord, saying, "O Lord, I will accept Your work." "Be ye not as the horse, or as the mule, which have no understanding" (Ps. 32.9a), failing to recognize the messages and disciplinary works of God. It is possible that you may be in God's hand for five or ten years and yet remain unbroken.

Today may you see His hand and submit yourself to it. Being broken, you will be softened and will no longer be self-righteous and self-absorbed. You will no longer look upon yourself as more than what you really are. This is truly being broken. Then your spirit will be released and you will begin to use it. Your spirit will also be open to receive all the supply of the spirit. Never try, therefore, to be tender and without self-love and self-righteousness before you submit yourself under the mighty hand of God. For doing so can be likened to trying to be justified by works. All who try to imitate will have one more layer of self to be broken. Just yield yourself to the discipline of the

Holy Spirit and accept His work. For as the outward man is broken the inward man will be strengthened: so unlike in the past, wherein the inward man was unable to be strong because of the strength of the outward man.

Let us see that the breaking of the outward man is most basic, for if the spirit is not serviceable no spiritual service can be done.[*]

---

[*]Note: Message *probably* spoken on April 22, 1949.

Chapter 10

FURTHER TALKS

(1) When personal guidance and body guidance differ, this is the time to wait. The word of the church may be accepted as the discipline of the Holy Spirit. What needs to be done when individual opinion and opinion of authority clash? Remember, authority is not for control but for building up. Today something may happen to me that I must wait for two or three years before it can be settled. The Lord uses authority to keep us from making mistakes. A brother who has walked in this way of the Lord for only five years may be able to do what another brother has done who has walked in the way for thirty years. Such is the effect of submitting to authority. Authority is a ministry, authority is for supply. Authority may be mistaken. When authority is right, I receive supply. When authority is wrong, I accept discipline. Submitting to authority may either result in the gain of supply or the reception of discipline. Both give spiritual blessing.

(2) The work done by the outpouring of the Holy Spirit and the work done through brokenness are not the same. Outpouring is one way in service, while brokenness is another way in serving. The Holy Spirit uses two channels for His release: one is by way of outpouring and the other is through a broken or contrite spirit. What is "outpouring"? The outpouring of the Holy Spirit is the pouring out of the Holy Spirit upon man's body. The power of many preachers does not come from the breaking of the outward

man but from the power of the Holy Spirit resting on them. When I speak, the Holy Spirit comes upon the sinners. This is possible to a beginner in the Lord. In order to supply the need of beginners, the Holy Spirit comes down, pours out upon them and gives them gifts. This enables the beginner to speak the word and save souls. Nevertheless, this becomes a problem to young people in that they suppose this is all there is about the Holy Spirit. The truth is — this is neither God's purpose nor His normal way. The church in its early days is full of gifts, but towards the end gifts seem to subside and dealing with the outward man becomes God's way. We believe the latter is the normal way of God. For He does not expect His people to depend on gifts for their entire life; rather, the eternal principle of His working lies in the need to have broken men and women. Gift is a temporary substitute for brokenness.

From the time of the Lord's crucifixion to the feast of Pentecost, the population in the city of Jerusalem was about one million. At the time of the apostles, the believers came to number three thousand and then five thousand. Each and every worker was accountable first to the Lord and then to himself. If people got helped, they were helped by the extra grace of the Lord, not by the workers themselves.

Outpouring is a prelude to brokenness. It is not a substitute. With people whose outward man is broken, they will bear fruits abundant and lasting. Everything needs to be put in its proper place. Outpouring is God's emergency measure. Suppose God saves twenty persons in a certain place. Of the twenty, none is able to edify the others. So, out of them God chooses one to edify the others, enabling him to say what he himself is yet ignorant of. The church is thereby edified. He who edifies others has more gift than grace. But due to his pride, he himself is not edified. God can use a donkey to help the prophet (see Num. 22.21-35), but the donkey is not therefore greater than the prophet. Many brethren know little about grace. Gift cannot be a substitute for grace. Outpouring may come suddenly, but brokenness requires years of discipline. Those who are gifted need to be humbled. They should see their "self" before God, not only work. How often has God used us as ass or used us as prophet? Be humble and be a truly broken vessel.

(3) We must resist all the works of the flesh, but we must not try to imitate the positive. Suppose a person is rude. The rudeness must be rejected, though gentleness should not be pretended. All works of the flesh must stop, but the positive character of gentleness is beyond imitation. For all the positive characteristics must be established in us by the Lord. The building up is through breaking down. Do not imitate nor pretend. We can be ignorant towards the existence of falsehood in our lives. Lying cheats oneself more than others. Imitation may deceive people for a time, but in the long run it deceives oneself. For he himself fails to know truth from falsity.

(4) Even what happens after making a mistake is also under government. Whenever an error is made, learn to submit to the discipline of God. The righteous person may suffer for keeping his oath. We all need to learn how to

submit ourselves under the mighty hand of God. After the princes of the congregation of Israel mistakenly swore by oath to the Gibeonites, they could not but keep the covenant which they had made with the Gibeonites (see Joshua 9.3-27). The children of Israel rebelled against God and were not allowed to enter the land of Canaan, even after their repentance (see Num. 14.39-45). After something was done wrongly, the people could indeed confess their sin at Kadesh-barnea, but they had to come under government.

If a vessel being worked upon is broken in the hand of the potter, it will be remade into a new vessel. Ask the Lord to make you a new vessel. Before the working of God's hand, things can be changed; but once God's hand moves, the only way left is to submit. For God will not stop till He is satisfied. How very serious is this matter.

(5) Even if we know that something came from Satan, it is nonetheless permitted by God. God has measured it, so we must submit. However, we must use our will to resist all which comes from Satan in spite of our accepting the arrangement of circumstance. We have the will to choose, and we choose what is God's. Whether or not God will move His hand depends on His own pleasure. Sometimes some brothers may be rather bad and yet they do not fall under discipline; but some other brothers who are not so bad fall into the disciplining hand of God. Why is this so? This is because according to the Scriptures it seems that the meting out of discipline is according to God's estimate of one's capacity. God will mete out upon us a little bit more discipline than our capacity so that we may learn to

endure. This is to increase our capacity. Government and discipline are not the same.

(6) Will the release of the spirit be affected by its objective? The spirit can be likened to a dove, for like the dove it comes forth to find a resting place. The spirit is unable to be released if it is deprived of such a situation. When a message is delivered, seventy to eighty percent of the responsibility for its outcome rests on the speaker, whereas the other twenty to thirty percent falls upon the audience. Nonetheless, it is different in gospel preaching, for our spirit should be able to overcome the resistance of sinners.

Mistakes committed through ignorance are also permitted by God. People are full of historical ideas. How much better if Adam had never sinned. But God lives in His glory. There are mountains and valleys; but when the entire earth is covered with water, these high mountains and low valleys become irrelevant. To us a lawyer turned physician is a big event, but in the eyes of God these two persons are the same. God receives the same glory as long as His purpose for you is reached.

Government makes all things work together for good. It leads the sons into glory. Government always leads to glory. On the one hand we must try to be careful lest we err; on the other hand, in spite of a thousand wrongs, God is still able to bring us into His eternal purpose which is glory. Anyhow, we are in the hand of the Lord. His glory shall fill the earth. Let us therefore commit ourselves into the Lord's hand (see John 10) and be fully aware of how awful it is to fall into the hand of God (see Heb. 10.26-31).[*]

---

[*] Note: Message given on April 22, 1949.

Part Two:

The Pattern of Sound Words

"Hold the pattern of sound words which thou hast heard from me, in faith and love which is in Christ Jesus."

II Timothy 1.13

GOD'S PURPOSE IN SAVING US

God's purpose in saving us is manifested through the breaking of our outward man; for the measure of the release of the spirit is according to the degree of the breaking of the outward man. There are several things which are most important to a Christian:

The removal of all obstacles that hinder us from having the presence of God and from being enlightened to know the mind of God;

The ability to experience true fellowship with the children of God;

The release of life in the preaching of the gospel through the pouring out of the inward man;

The ministry of God's word through the release of the spirit.

None of the above items is possible without the outward man being broken by God. Our constitution is two-fold: on the one side is what comes from Adam, and on the other side is what is being built in us through the years. From the time we are saved and regenerated we have the Spirit of the Lord dwelling in our human spirit. This is the inward man. It is born of the Spirit, and it is spirit. Thus, our original man from before regeneration becomes the outward man. The Lord's purpose is to break down our outward man day after day till we see the Lord.

THE RELATION BETWEEN
THE INWARD AND OUTWARD MAN

"That which is born of the Spirit is spirit"

Whatever is born of the Spirit is spirit (see John 3.6b). However, at first this spirit in us is not independent, but is attached to the outward man. It is therefore restricted by the outward man, thus conducting itself according to the outward man. The purity of the spirit comes from the breaking of the outward man. Prior to breaking, the outward man gives the spirit its feature or characteristic. However, should the characteristic of the outward man be broken, the inward becomes unfettered and is now a free spirit, having its independent life. It is no longer supported by the outward man but is now able to live independently through the Lord. So, even at the time of a person's old age, although memory may fail, thought may falter and strength may decline, it is but the hour to reveal how much God has built in him and how much has been broken.

A grain of wheat falls into the ground and dies, and it bears much fruit. This refers to the breaking of the outer shell to allow the seed to bud (see John 12.24). If any man loses himself (his soul life), he may keep his spirit life to eternity (cf. John 12.25). The outward man — the soul or the psychological man — includes our will, mind and emotion. After the outward man is broken, one may touch the presence of God. Without the breaking of the outward man no one can truly serve God. We therefore need to put ourselves in His hand, willing to be broken under His arrangement. Without denying self no one can follow the Lord. May the Lord be increased and I be decreased. May I take up the cross and follow Him.

Our initial consecration must be thorough and absolute; otherwise, we cannot bear the trials. Then, in order to walk well, we must maintain an absolute surrender, a solid consecration, joyfully accepting the discipline of the Holy Spirit. Consecration marks the beginning; the discipline of the Holy Spirit will follow. All our happenings are arranged by the Lord. They all are for the breaking of our outward man. Let us learn to receive such breaking in all circumstances day by day that we may be broken more and more.

The Target of Breaking

What is the target of breaking? A person who is overly rich in emotion will find that the release of his spirit is being restricted due to his emotion. Thus, such emotion becomes a target of breaking. The highest expression of a Christian life is purity. Outward emotion should be used by the inward man without being mixed with the characteristic of the outward man. The reason for the Spirit's discipline is because of our impurity — the mixing in of the outward man — which prevents us from walking after the inward spirit. We must therefore ask God to break down our outward man. This is the key. It is most basic.

Our emotion may either give the spirit a free way of release or maintain its independence and stand at the opposite side of the spirit. Hence, from the day we are saved the Lord begins to break down our outward man. This is the discipline of the Holy Spirit. He knows the need of our inward man much more than we would even want to know. He arranges the most suitable environment for us, causing our inward man to grow and our outward man to be broken. The latter is being broken step by step. Each breaking is more advanced than the previous breaking. The Lord is wounding our outward man till we are truly broken. He works until we let go of ourselves.

A Christian should inwardly choose to walk in his inner path (that is, according to the inward man). Indeed, he will find himself being outwardly disciplined by the hand of the Lord to travel in this path. It is natural for man to love self. Yet our Lord has not just commanded us to not love self; He also takes a further step of breaking down our self-love till we have no way to love self. Such is the discipline of God as manifested in our environment. We should learn to say, "We are open to anything from the Lord as well as open to anything from men." The most regretful situation is to have learned nothing under dealing.

Pride is the sin of the will. Many consider themselves superior, higher and better than other people. A proud person often thinks of himself; he always taking notice of himself. This is pride. His self is the center of everything. God must break down such people. The work of the Holy Spirit in us is not only manifested in supplying us with the word of God but also in the arrangement of our environment. Only a fool will resist the discipline of the Holy Spirit. It is impossible to grow by hearing God's word alone; we must also learn to submit to His special arrangement in circumstances. Never neglect the arrangement of environment. Even the supply of the word is part of God's special arrangement. We need to understand the way which the Lord has set before us. May we all confess, "O Lord, I am truly willing to submit to Your mighty hand!"

Such seeing is most practical. We need to see why there must be the breaking of the outward man. Every day, as it were, we are in school; daily the Lord is teaching us. The discipline of the Holy Spirit is everywhere. He works incessantly till one day the inward man, the outward man and the outside environment no longer clash. Not till then will a Christian have real peace. Such will be the glorious day, the joyous day, and the greatest day. We will thank God, for everything will then speak of peace, joy and power.

To know is a great thing. God has given light by which to see that all is of the Lord. In this light many problems are solved. How often we forget God and either see men or see things. Yet trying to suppress ourselves is also wrong. We must be clear within and our eyes must be enlightened. Once our eyes are opened we will not quarrel with Pilate or the Romans. Instead, we will say, "O Father! How can I not drink the cup that You have given me?" Do not just be a hearing Christian, seeking growth through the supply of God's word alone, for this is only half of our experience. Be aware of the disciplinary arrangement of the Lord; for once we are enlightened, it is easy to accept discipline. As the light shines we bow our heads and pray, "O Lord! I praise You." It really does not matter much if there is the lack of the supply of God's word; but we cannot live without the discipline of the Holy Spirit. Therefore, seek to know the hand of the Lord. Thus shall we be greatly blessed. The effect of discipline is great. The supply of the word on the one hand and the discipline of the Holy Spirit on the other — this is real Christianity.

Because these two work together, take special notice of where the Lord strikes hard; that is, discover the target upon which the hand of the Lord hits. Such understanding gives birth to a true minister of the word. This can be considered a "professional" secret. Light is in the hand of the minister, coming on the one hand out of his inner sense and on the other hand from observing the outside arrangement of the Holy Spirit. Then, the ministry of the word can work with the light to break down the outward part of man.

Preaching the Gospel and Brokenness

What is the relationship between gospel preaching and brokenness? The aim of preaching the gospel is that people's spirits might be quickened by my spirit. Such quickening never comes through good exposition of doctrine. Indeed, neither the teaching given in Acts 2, Stephen's word in Acts 7, Peter's message in the house of Cornelius in Acts 10 nor Paul's preaching of the gospel in some later chapters in Acts can be reckoned as crystal clear. Yet people's hearts were pricked and many got saved after hearing; for the secret of getting people saved lies not in the teaching but in the preachers. Under the teachings of the Lord for three and a half years the twelve apostles received many instructions of both an outward and inward nature. Peter was representative of these twelve. The Lord said to Peter, "Verily I say unto thee, that this night, before the cock crow, thou shalt deny me thrice" (Matt. 26.34). This marks the lowest point in Peter's life.

What is meant by the baptism in the Holy Spirit? It is when God by His mighty power lays hold of a person's spirit to do the work of quickening his spirit. Such is the baptism in the Holy Spirit. Today my spirit can be released to teach and quicken the spirit of another. So, whether the spirit can be released is all that matters. From reading the book by the Scottish evangelist James M'Kendrick mentioned previously,[*] it becomes quite evident that he was not an eloquent preacher, but his spirit was able to be released far more than his spoken word. He could be likened to water that gushes forth, not as water that freezes up. He deeply sensed the danger of man's future and was terribly concerned. His zealous spirit rushed out as a torrent, arousing people's conscience. A frozen person is unable to preach the gospel, for the spirit of a hard heart cannot be released. In such a case there is absolutely no way to quicken the spirit of another.

Alas, today we are short of time for God to do this breaking work within us. When we begin to preach the gospel, on the one hand let us ask the Lord to open up that basic way of brokenness to us, and on the other hand learn

---

[*] See Chapter 5 above, p. 48.

to resist or shut up our own thought and feeling lest we perform out from ourselves. It is the "real honey" that really attracts the bees. Do not pretend and act. Do not lean on your own thought and feeling. Learn to speak within the limit of the weight or burden of the words within your spirit. Ignore your outward man. Do not be mindful of the reaction of other people. Whatever words you have within, speak accordingly. Never allow your outward man to interfere with your inward man. Let the burden within be released. Never mind what others may think or feel. If the word requires weeping, weep; if it demands kneeling, then kneel; if it asks for shouting, shout. The inward man must not be bound. It should be free to be released. This is of great importance.

Preaching the gospel with restraint will restrain people from getting saved. The power of gospel preaching rests on the ability to send out the words by the inward man. Gradually we shall discern the burden in our spirit and the approach that the Spirit would have us take. People get saved when they meet the spirit of the gospel.

Brokenness is a work of a lifetime. Yet there is no need to wait until after death to be totally broken. For its climax may be quickly realized by the obedient. Such a person can quickly be broken. After his fall, Peter lost his confidence of loving the Lord. He was now a broken person. "Verily, verily, I say unto thee, When thou wast young, thou girdest thyself, and walkedst whither thou wouldest: but when thou shalt be old, thou shalt stretch forth thy hands, and another shall gird thee, and carry thee whither thou wouldest not" (John 21.18). This pointed to how Peter would die. From this we can see that the current climax in Peter's life was not the end, for "Whither thou wouldest not" still speaks of future brokenness. How much does one need to be broken before he can be used by the Lord? There is no absolute rule or standard. Yet one must be broken to a certain extent. Peter was not conscious of his usefulness, he had no confidence in his work. Indeed, confidence of work lies not in the estimation of the servant but in the estimation of the Master. In fact, it was not until shortly before his death that Peter wrote his epistles in which he realized that in shepherding the flock of God's people he sensed death in himself yet resurrection in the work.

None serving the Lord has confidence in himself. We all sense death and yet how resurrection works. Peter was a person who sensed deeply his failure in tending the lambs of the Lord. Spirituality never gives us a feeling of confidence or boldness. In the light of the Lord many of our difficulties are being dealt with; in the meanwhile we keep on working. We feel inadequate and still we labor on. It is only in serving that the measure of brokenness is shown. A person who is broken should always serve feeling meek and disabled. Due to brokenness, he learns to do some spiritual work through the Lord. Yet while serving he always feels weak and crucified, though he is raised to power in resurrection. Peter was not clear, but the Lord was clear, and the church was clear. He alone was unclear. When the climax comes, you begin to go forward step by step. There is no sense of having graduated. You do not know how much you have to learn, before the Lord is willing to trust you. You do not know, but the Lord knows and His church also knows. May the Lord lead our steps to those who have been ordained to eternal life. Pray much that we do not waste our effort.

In preaching the gospel to sinners we need to give them enough knowledge. Our preconceived idea can be a hindrance to helping people. A basic rule for preaching the gospel is never be subjective; use as little teaching as is necessary. Remember this rule: save first, and then teach. Teaching too much may make salvation more difficult. Learn to be a meek person, a man who is being broken and who is becoming wise. Preach to a certain degree and then stop. The breaking of the outward man is mainly seen in God's control of our inordinate thoughts. We dare not touch our own ideas. The more a person is broken the simpler he becomes. Thus the strength in his spirit is preserved for use at its right moment. Speaking carelessly and thinking wildly are signs of unbrokenness in a person, whereas the one who is broken dares not think or speak for fear of making a mistake. Such a person's mind is under control and is duty-bound. He bears a very great responsibility before God.

God commits His word to His ministers. He entrusts the gospel into the hands of His people. We are therefore truly responsible lest we hinder the mighty work of God upon sinners. We are like people who spread garments in the way or cut branches from trees and spread them in the way (see Matt. 21.8, Mark 11.8, Luke 19.36). We must help people to be truly spread in the way for the Lord to pass through. The strength of the gospel depends on how

much we are able to be spread in the way, for people are
God's way. If the gospel can pass through the lives of the
children of God, then it will show its power in the lives of
sinners. The sinner's future depends on our condition today.
This generation must be planted so that the next generation
can spring up. May the Lord cause us to make an absolute
consecration that can withstand all temptation. Then shall
we see people more powerfully saved.

The Christian Way Is Spiritual

The Christian way is a spiritual way. Putting it another
way, whatever things are done without spirit or that cannot
release the spirit should not be done, for they are
meaningless. The humility which proceeds from within has
the spirit because it is the result of the moving of the Lord
from within us. Mere outward exhibition has not the spirit.
Only what comes out of the spirit gives supply, for it is
neither manufactured nor pretended. It is difficult for
people to receive what is not given by the release of the
spirit. Christian life is not measured by outside action but
all depends on whether there is the spirit within the action.
Here lies the greatest difference. Without the breaking of
the outward man your spirit will not be released. With the
spirit blocked there can be no life supply. All is dead. They
all are dead works: dead gentleness, dead humility, dead
love, dead faith. All manifestations without the spirit are
altogether dead. On the other hand, people will see, from
the living actions done out of the spirit, the person who has
been stricken by God. You should not look at a brother's
actions and try to imitate him. Do not put on the face of a

seminary student and try to imitate someone spiritual. In so doing you begin to deceive others, and will eventually deceive yourself. Do not add more manufactured things to your life only to wait for God to destroy them. This is inevitable, for without having these things destroyed, God's word will have no real way to be released from you. From the perspective of the church, such a self-manufactured person is like a corpse.

When the spirit is released it produces two different effects on people. When the outward man has been broken it gives the spirit a sense of spiritual echo (or spiritual response). However, it also will have a spiritual impact on others. For the spirit is for service as well as for daily living. Church service consists of one spirit touching another spirit and then returning to the first one. Thus they supply each other. It can be likened to atomic movement which produces kinetic energy. When my spirit is released and touches others, my spirit is also being moved. This is being edified. God is not partial to anyone. In His church each and every one can learn to serve Him in spirit. Whenever there is spirit, it is right. Whatever is without spirit is always wrong.

Nothing can be accomplished if what has been built up outwardly is not destroyed. Here is the difference between us and the world. Here lies the difference between the spiritual and the carnal. Our way is in brokenness, not in outward up-building. This age is becoming more and more materialistic. Our way lies in discerning the spirit. Otherwise, how can we resist when great trial comes? He who has the Holy Spirit has Christ; he that has not the Holy Spirit has not Christ.

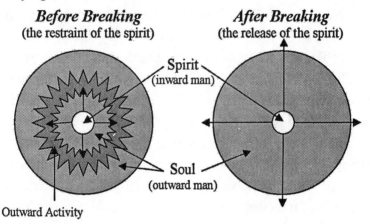

Before Breaking
(the restraint of the spirit)

After Breaking
(the release of the spirit)

Spirit
(inward man)

Soul
(outward man)

Outward Activity

"Through the breaking of the outward man all outward activity is destroyed..."

"... in order that the spirit might be released and what cannot be destroyed might remain."

Through the breaking of the outward man all outward action is destroyed in order that the spirit might be released and what cannot be destroyed might remain. We usually will not gladly accept the circumstances which the Lord has arranged for our brokenness, for we consider them to be painful and unpleasant. Yet, since God wants to break us and grind us as fine meal, we must not resist His will. The moment we fall down before God people will touch our spirit.

It is true that the spirit of a newly regenerated person may be released quite easily, yet it is always tainted with characteristics of the outward man. The water of a hot spring that has passed through a mineral mine has many chemicals melted in it, and hence, it is impure. On the other hand, the water on Mount Kuling does not contain any melted minerals; therefore, it is very sweet and pure. When the spirit is released without any mixture, then can it be called "living water"; for when it flows out and touches people, it gives spiritual supply. The release of the spirit without the mixture of the outward man within it demands the breaking of the outward man. With the latter being broken, we then become clear channels; otherwise, the spirit will remain buried and things other than the spirit will flow out.

What are some of the things which *can* flow out? Rich thoughts may help the inward spirit. Even man's emotion may also be used by the spirit. But these are the things which remain after having gone through the breaking, wounding process. All else must be eliminated, for God will use nothing which comes out of man's self-life: neither the wisdom of the wise nor the foolishness of the fool. The Lord will distribute to His servants according to their several ability. To one He gives one talent, to another He gives two talents, and to still another He gives five talents. From the perspective of man's history before God, he has been set apart at least in his mother's womb. It does not depend on our reckoning but on God's call. When the mother gives birth to a child, God distributes to each his special ability. Then, at the time of service, He arranges to each his talent according to His thought.

In service and in the preaching of the gospel, whether we do it rightly or wrongly, we must do it; for this is commanded in the Bible. It is always good to serve and to preach the gospel. However, in order to do it rightly or at a

minimum do it with less wrong, we need to lay hold of two
things: believing the church and trusting the Holy Spirit. In
practice, we need to learn humility, learning to accept any
correction from the church. We also need to learn to take
note of the resistance of the Holy Spirit and trust in His
discipline. In the book of Acts there are more instances of
"forbidden of the Holy Spirit" than "leading of the Holy
Spirit." Therefore, let us learn to submit ourselves to the
discipline of the Holy Spirit. In instances where there is
fear of the opposition of Satan, it needs the confirmation of
the church. So, the way of service is preaching on the one
hand and learning on the other. Work as much as learn.
The Holy Spirit will begin to use us in the shortest possible
time. Pentecost marks the beginning of the Church, not her
end. Since the Church began at Pentecost, she grows richer
and richer with the abundance of Christ. The Lord makes
us serviceable on the one hand and perfect on the other.
Thus are we being brought fully to the Lord.

Love arising from self is self-centered and selfish. In
himself man never really loves another person. Sometimes
he may seem to love, but actually such "love" is rooted in
an expectation to be loved. Human love is a kind of power
in men but it is limited. It is like the limitation of the
weight which a man is able to bear. You love one and you
are thus unable to love another. All who serve God need to
be rid of such self-love, for by loving self they are unable
to love God and man. How very pitiful is this matter of
self-love. It blocks the way to love others. Realizing the
frailty of the power of love, let us use it with care. All who
serve God will have been delivered from this self-love.

Many expect to be loved, and when they fail to get it they begin to love self and feel nobody treats them well. May God have mercy on us and rid us of this self-love. For the self-loved, the discipline of the Holy Spirit is hard to take. They try to hide from it, and the discipline becomes more severe. Alas, many still fail to recognize the sin of self-love. How blessed is he who recognizes the hand of God in this area and falls under His hand without further struggle.

Dealing with the Conscience

Any dealing with conscience will reduce the hindrance to the spirit. This is also included in the disciplinary works of God. The dealings against sins and unrighteousness will grow in scope, and the understanding and sense of righteousness (for to be one with God is a matter of righteousness) will advance continuously. Things which we should not know and yet seek to know are also unrighteous, for we gain understanding beyond our right. There needs to be real growth in the recognition of righteousness. Towards this end the Holy Spirit will arrange our trials day by day. As a result we begin to learn to resist every unrighteous thought. In this way we do not need to wait until there is actual sin before we deal with it, for we have already dealt with it in our conscience. However, conscience itself also needs to be purified. Although confession will soften the outward man, it is growth in the discerning of righteousness which will reveal how much the believer has learned.

The word "consecration" in Hebrew places more emphasis on God's acceptance than on how much we may offer up. All the offerings in the Old Testament rest on the blood. They should not be considered as our respectful acts of piety. The emphasis of consecration is on the acceptance of God. How we often consider it to be the giving of something to God. In the book of Job, Job cries out, "Behold, if he slay me, yet would I trust in him" (13.15 Darby). This is the most severe test. In the third chapter of Job we see how Job began to murmur due to his illness. But a truly consecrated person can overcome it, for all chastenings are done for the sake of producing the fruit of holiness (see Heb. 12.9-10). The trial of fire brings in purity. Then will we realize its value. The real meaning of consecration is reflected in our saying, "O Lord! I truly desire after You. I really want to give my all to You." If anyone does not have such consecration, he needs to have it so.

Is your consecration like that of Peter? When he expressed his heart to the Lord, it revealed the boldness of his flesh. He had confidence in himself that he would never forsake the Lord. Yet later on, he fell terribly before a maid. Then, coming back after being defeated, he prostrated himself before the Lord, saying, "O Lord! You know I love You, though I dare not say it now." This attitude can serve as a remedy to your sinful consecration, and this is also the correct way. Simon Peter confessed before the Lord, saying, "I know my consecration is undependable, but Lord, I want to love You." This one who had fallen before a maid was the same Peter who later challenged all the inhabitants in Jerusalem on the day of Pentecost declaring: "Let all the house of Israel therefore know assuredly, that

God hath made him both Lord and Christ, this Jesus whom ye crucified" (Acts 2.36).

How many people at their first consecration have done so with great pride according to their flesh! Then, as soon as they are tested, they fall. For consecration must embody not only a heart of consecration that is perfect but also an attitude of consecration that is humble. The attitude of humility is, "If You, Lord, will accept" — this is grace. Tell the Lord, "I have nothing to offer, but I still love You. If I could only touch the skirt of Your garment, it is enough." I have no need to touch the Lord's hands or feet.

In our environment there are many things which come from the attacks of Satan. In the New Testament only the epistles of James and Peter tell us that we should resist Satan. It is also these two letters which tell us how we must submit ourselves under the mighty hand of God (that is, His disciplinary hand). To Satan we always say, "No"; to the Lord we always say, "Yes." With respect to the things we submit to the Lord we tell Satan: "We will resist you." But for the one who does not submit himself under the mighty hand of God he cannot resist Satan with a restful conscience. Oftentimes, instead of resisting Satan we resist God. Yet, as we resist Satan on the one hand and praise God on the other, there is real peace.

Submission under the mighty hand of God is a basic requirement. Deep in my heart I must confess that I am not here suffering but rather am here submitting myself to God, while at the same time I exercise my faith to resist the enemy. All things are done under the principle of submission, for every movement in our daily living comes from the discipline of the Holy Spirit. If the inner eye of man is clear, he may always discern the discipline of the Holy Spirit. Such a one has no need to wait till a heavy wind blows or the house is hit.

We must have a sensitive spirit and enlightened eyes lest we miss the discipline of the Holy Spirit. All happenings which come from the discipline of the Spirit are meaningful, whereas all which comes from Satan is void of any meaning, for such merely causes us to suffer and be troubled. Let us inquire of the Lord, "O Lord! What is the reason, after all?" The Lord will quickly show us that whatever things come from Satan are altogether meaningless. So, you should immediately say to Satan, "Whatever comes from the Lord I will submit to; but whatever comes from you, I will resist." As you resist, Satan will flee from you. May God teach us this lesson.

All our prayers need to be truthful. This is the first principle of prayer. Do not imitate the way others speak. Nor are you to make your thoughts known through prayer, for you are not praying to people. Your inner inspiration should not be blocked by the outward man. Yet the greatest problem in prayer is: many words but little burden. In order for prayer to be answered, two things are necessary. First, there must be no obstruction of sin. Conscience needs to be dealt with. If there are holes in the conscience, the vessel of faith will sink. You must at least deal with the sins you already know. You have no need to search for sins. You are only responsible for those you know. All such sins must be covered with the precious blood of the Lord.

Second, you must pray specifically for the thing you pray for and pray with simple faith. What is faith? When you pray, believe that you have received what you pray for and you shall thereby receive (see Mark 11.24 margin). Continuing to pray for a particular matter after having such faith causes you to lose your faith. Before you have faith, you pray; after you have faith, you praise. When the children of Israel were in the wilderness, they believed and then they praised. And so, they immediately received.

Three Stages of Consecration

The consecration of the children of God may be divided into three stages. During the first stage there is always the sense of being incomplete and of a lack of absoluteness. Even though I have a heart to give myself to the Lord Jesus, there remains in me the reluctance of going all the way. Then, during the second stage, a revival comes. This may be caused by the discipline of the Holy Spirit or through the supply of the word of God, and results in a more thorough consecration to the Lord. At that time I have the assurance that my consecration is absolute, and have confidence that I am wholly for the Lord. Yet, when I encounter heavier discipline and breaking in that stage, I fall terribly, thus proving that my consecration is undependable. Nevertheless, even though my pride breaks down at that time, my consecration remains intact. At the third stage the consecration is in fact complete, though one may still feel incomplete and thus filled with fear and trembling; for the completeness of consecration is never one of feeling. To be filled with the Holy Spirit is not a matter of self-consciousness. We are conscious of not being filled by the Holy Spirit, but we will never know subjectively when we are filled with the Holy Spirit.

Moses' shining face was not to be seen by him but was for the children of Israel to see. The fact of consecration is there, but in feeling you will say to the Lord, "O Lord! I shortchange You. I am undone, my consecration is still less than one tenth." In fact, we will always maintain a kind of reservation in asserting our consecration. After Peter denied the Lord thrice, three times he later on dared not say to the Lord that he loved Him. His arrogance had been completely smashed. We need to be strong in God but weak in our feeling. God performs many works in men, yet not according to man's self-assurance but according to what He has foreordained.

According to the fourth and fifth chapters of the Letter to the Ephesians, the Church will grow into the full stature of Christ, without spot or wrinkle or any of such things. Once a person's consecration is complete he will eventually be led by God to the place of a perfect member of the body of Christ, thus manifesting the glory of God. God's way for today is the ministry of the church, and the preaching of the gospel by the church is to be led by the Holy Spirit. If a church is open to God, the stream of the Holy Spirit will come; we will just follow. After a while, another stream will come, and we again follow on. If the worker is able to follow the flow, blessed is he.

With regard to signs accompanying the ministry of God's word, eighty percent of miracles happen in the villages, they seeming to stop at the city gate. We learn in the book of Acts that the apostles did not perform many miracles in Jerusalem, and the many miracles performed by Paul also took place in the villages. Although speaking in tongues (using the spirit without using the mind) is mentioned in 1 Corinthians 14, Paul advocated using both spirit and mind in preaching. According to the same letter, if the tongue is not being interpreted, it is better not to speak.

The dealing of the Holy Spirit and the accusation of Satan are fundamentally different in several ways. First, when the Holy Spirit reproaches us, He always gives us a clear sense of what He wants us to know and to do. Satan is totally different in his approach and is like a gossiping woman uttering indistinctly. The Holy Spirit never mumbles. His indication is always distinct and compelling.

When the Holy Spirit makes known to you your sin, you will be enlightened in your heart. This is the reproach of the Holy Spirit that needs to be immediately dealt with. Satan, however, does not give you any clear understanding. He only tries to disturb you. You should confess to God because you are wrong, not because you feel uncomfortable. Never fall into the trap of Satan who tries to paralyze you. Should you confess because you feel uncomfortable, you play into his hand, causing you to waste your time and become confused. Do not ever confess carelessly in order to gain peace within.

After confession, if you have peace and joy, or at least have peace, then it is of God. But if the accusation comes from Satan, you will still be disturbed even after prayer, for his motive is to trouble you; he has no desire to make you holy. In this matter of confession, there is the need of both light and the blood of Jesus. If a confession depends only on light, your conscience will be hurt; but with the blood comes forgiveness and peace in the conscience. You need to have the blood on the one hand and the light on the other. Neither can be missing.

A consecrated heart prays, "I lay my day in Your hand. Lead me to those whose hearts have been prepared by You." For the Lord alone knows where the fish are. When His net is cast, there are one hundred and fifty-three fish caught (see John 21.5-6, 10-11).

Consecration marks the beginning of God's discipline. In the plan of God, a person who has truly consecrated himself will begin to experience the discipline of the Holy Spirit. This will be more and more distinctive as he goes on. Before this time, the work of the Holy Spirit is solely to lead us to consecration.

In the three stages of consecration, discipline and the ministry of God's word are in inverse proportion; that is, the more the word, the less the need of discipline. The more the word is received, the less the ordering of circumstance is needed. God always works in such a way as to bring many things in the lives of Christians to naught. Such are the lives of God's children. Though the proportion of the word and the discipline varies, the sum total is the same.

Due to the brokenness brought about through the Lord's word, discipline may be reduced. Acceptance of God's word and obedience to it may reduce the need of being broken by the arrangement of circumstances. Yet it is he who receives more mercies who receives more dealings. He who receives less mercy receives less dealings. The quantity each receives differs. Be thankful for more dealings, for such dealings are evidence that the Lord has more hope in the life of such a one. Indeed, there are many who seem to miss God's mercy.

Live in the Inward Man

He whose outward man is broken lives by his inward man. Otherwise, he still lives by the outward man, and consequently his life remains unchanged. With the breaking of the outward man, a distance will be created between the inward and outward man. The two will then be disassociated. After the breaking of our outside shell by God, we will naturally bear the fruit of knowing His presence. Young people find themselves unable to continue in God's presence. Although they sometimes sense His nearness, most of the time they feel that He is at a distance. This is a most painful experience, and for this reason, many times they lose their peace. Although returning to God is a great phenomenon, it is also a painful experience. Only after our outward man is broken are we able to continue unceasingly in the presence of God.

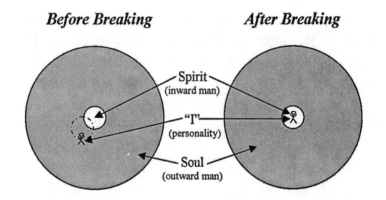

Before Breaking   *After Breaking*

The personality dwells in
either the inward man or the
outward man.

The personality dwells in the
inward man only.

The Problem with Personality – How Do I Live?

The secret of living continuously in the presence of
God lies in the breaking of the outward man. As a result of
this breaking, my personality will live no longer in the
outward man; for the latter has suffered a fatal blow, and
now my personality dwells in the inward man. As a result,
wonderful things begin to happen. You may be busily
engaged and yet you seem to be watching another being so
engaged, for your personality now dwells in the inward
man. Though the outward man is busy, the inward man
remains unmoved. It seems as though the inward man is
there watching the busyness of the outward man. Our
morning prayer starts our spiritual life for the day before
God. It should not require great effort to come before Him.
But in the evening when we return to God, it seems to be
quite difficult. Each time we experience such a sense of

returning, it proves that our presence with God has been interrupted. Hence, it seems difficult to return to God's presence. By contrast, our Lord Jesus could be angry without for a moment losing God's presence. Even anger will not produce any distance with God. With the breaking of the outward man we are enabled to abide in the inward man, and can look upon the busyness of the outward man as having been instructed by God to be so engaged. We can pray without being adversely affected. For many unfortunately, the inward and the outward are still undivided and they move as one unit. May God break our outward man, causing us not to return to our former life that needs to be corrected and adjusted by Him all day long.

"The word of God is living, and active, and sharper than any two-edged sword, and piercing even to the dividing of soul and spirit, of both joints and marrow, and quick to discern the thoughts and intents of the heart" (Heb. 4.12). The word of God is intensely living and effective upon us. When one day His word comes livingly to you, its light shines upon you, causing the dividing of soul and spirit. You fall under it; it is sufficient just to see what is revealed to you today. Light will reveal the bad "you" to you. How many things come out from yourself, and how few come from the spirit. Such revelation causes you to be so ashamed of yourself that you immediately fall to the ground. Your outward man is paralyzed. This is all you need. It is a great day for you; henceforth, you are unable to get up again. In your eyes, there is nothing more ugly than your outward man. There remains no more strength in you. Hereafter you are totally useless. May God open our eyes to see our self.

The Enlightenment and the Discipline of the Holy Spirit

The lack of the discipline of the Holy Spirit today is due to the shortage of consecration in the church. There are also people who love their own selves to the extreme, and whose shells are so hard that their spirits cannot be released. These people consider themselves as having no difficulty in the preaching of the gospel, in the ministry of the word, and in fellowship. Also, there are those proud persons who consider themselves superior. They go everywhere to teach others, yet they have no piety towards God and are careless in their lives. Furthermore, there are also those who never learn from the discipline of their environment.

With regard to the enlightenment of the Holy Spirit, light may come through prayer, but it can also be lost through prayer. When we are under the flow of the Holy Spirit yet continue to pray for His flow, we will instantly lose it. This follows the same principle as other types of prayer. Before being enlightened we should pray for light that we may receive the supply of the word. But after we have received the word, we should humble ourselves before it. We should not continue to ask lest we lose the word. Who would light a lamp once the sun has risen?

Under the light there is no possibility of being lenient with oneself, perplexed or unsure of one's motives. Everything becomes clear, and we are able to discern what comes from our selves. Through God's mercy light shines upon all things. The light makes all the difference. Under enlightenment we can detect evil even in our best intent. Such discernment is basic and is absolutely needed. How often sin is mere terminology in our lives. But under the scrutiny of light sin becomes truly sinful. Formerly there was confession according to mental knowledge, but now it is confession according to God's judgment. This is called the judgment of light. Light will also discern all the thoughts and intents of the heart, causing you to see how little is truly for the Lord and how much is really for yourself. As the light shines upon a man he immediately falls down. At that time it is no longer a matter of asking for enlightenment but a matter of immediately falling down. It is absolutely useless trying to fall down by ourselves. Light is God's power to smash and to tear down. No one is able to stand under revelation, for all is broken down. There is only one step in revelation, unlike listening to God's word and doing it — which involves two steps. Revelation is our salvation.

The cross in the Bible points to this enlightenment of God. Merely having the light of knowledge causes pride, because it builds up self. However, seeing the true light humbles you and wounds the self. Insufficient light fails to break you and instead makes self even more active than before. Hence, the need is for more severe basic enlightenment. Such basic treatment is thorough and humbling.

The Release of the Spirit

The breaking of the outward man leaves an undeniable mark on our lives in order that throughout our lives we can never forget what the hand of the Lord has done in us. We will not fail to see that all which we do according to our selves has no spiritual value and needs to be broken. The work of the Holy Spirit on the one hand is revelation and on the other hand is the breaking of the outward man through His arrangement of our environment. Such revelation causes us to see and to fall down. What is to be feared in such "seeing" is that it may only become an ornament for self and will thus build up our pride. If so, we shall become more and more confident of ourselves. This is improper and must be avoided. For true spiritual seeing will never make us proud of ourselves but will cause us to lose our pride.

Such a humble seeing is a must for young people. Whether it be like Peter going through failure or like Paul paralyzed under great light, each and every Christian must have such an experience. The true Christian life is not reckoned as beginning from the day of repentance and acceptance of the Lord, for from the day of regeneration to the time of falling down before the Lord only marks the beginning of a Christian. True Christian life commences from the day of falling down before the Lord because only then do we realize the lordship of Christ. Delaying this commencement is a waste of time. We must redeem our time before God. Time is a big issue, for we do not know how long the Church may freely serve the Lord.

Today I commit you all to the grace of the Holy Spirit, passing on to you His way in revelation and the breaking brought about through His arrangement of circumstances. This can be brought about in no other way. May we entertain no secret controversy or murmuring against God in these things. Shall I not drink the cup that my Father has given me? I have yet to see God ever choosing one who merely has the outward appearance of Christ. God always breaks us thoroughly.

God's children possess the special characteristic of being risen from among the dead just as their Lord Jesus, who has the nail scars in His hands and the spear wound on His side. For all real resurrection life bears wounds. An untouched life is useless. God cannot use one who is saved but who is without any breaking from Him. The foundation of ministry and the extent of being His servant rests upon how many wounds one possesses in life. An untouched life shows no wound. The apostle Paul bore in his body the marks of Jesus (see Gal. 6.17).

To serve God requires our having wounds. When a person with wounds touches others, they will meet one who knows the Lord. On the other hand, they are not able to be touched by someone who can preach but has never been stricken by God. An unbroken person may give the impression of being moral in the eyes of the world, but among Christians he merely shows forth the flesh. Everyone should bear the wounds of Christ. This is not for the sake of showing forth what light has done in us; rather, it testifies that we have been dealt with. We dare not be proud or careless. In this way we live as Christians. We are the product of enlightenment and environmental arrangement. Let us walk in this way, gladly allowing God to accomplish such work in us. He who carries in his body the wounds of Christ has his outward man broken. This also enables him to have real fellowship among the brethren. Many cannot release their spirit and as a result hide themselves among the brothers and sisters. So, in fellowshiping it is essential that we not have contact about doctrine only. There must be the touching of spirit. Without having wounds on the outside shell, life will not be able to flow forth. Do not keep people from touching your spirit; rather, let your spirit be released that others may be fed. Learning and knowledge undealt with are useless in the church. What is useful in the church is the spirit.

Do not despise the unlearned and the poor, for in fact they may learn more than you do. The one who is broken is able both to release his spirit and to receive more help. Many of God's children lack the power of discernment. But if one is broken, all those whose spirits are pure will immediately respond; for they have the power of recognition in their spirit. With the breaking of the outward man, even your thoughts may manifest the feeling of the spirit. All your senses become usable. Your peace, your joy and all your feelings are carried out by the spirit, and the inward man will direct the outward man. As you deal with sinners according to the feeling of the inward man, the preaching of the gospel becomes easy.

Today, too often our way of living relies on memory and determination, while at other times it depends on self-control and feeling. But one day, memory and feeling will fail and self-control will also lose its strength. We will be unable to use our former prowess, but will have the sense of being aged. Indeed, when we are aging, our physical strength and mental power gradually weaken. It is then that it will be manifested what kind of Christian we are. What one has learned through God's dealings all through his life, and all his learning in the spirit, will be revealed. What has truly been recovered is what remains after the things learned when we were young begin to fade away. If the outward man is our life-style today, when we grow old, this earthen vessel will be fully exposed. All self-control will be gone. Then shall we realize what God has done in our lives.

Authority

All authority comes from God and is used for two purposes: service in the church and the discipline of the Holy Spirit. As to its first use, many have the mistaken idea of authority as forcing us to do what we do not wish to do. On the contrary, authority enables us to help the spiritually unlearned to submit themselves under the hands of the spiritually learned. In this way authority is exercised to help new believers minimize the time of learning in order that they may learn quickly what would usually take twenty years. It also saves them from many failures and errors. Hence, one who is obedient can save himself from many learning pains and much learning time. Rebellion is the greatest loss to the church. But when I walk in obedience, recognizing the Lord, authority becomes a help.

As to the second use, authority is also for the discipline of the Holy Spirit. At times authoritative command can be helpful. At the least it will not fail to serve as the discipline of the Holy Spirit. For He may use such authoritative command to our greatest advantage. Therefore, it is never wrong to learn submission to authority. The quicker the submission the more readily the benefit is reaped. Many times God will also begin to break down the external grace we learned earlier in order to deliver us from pride. A recognition of authority is one of the fundamental senses of a Christian. Seek God everywhere, also seek authority everywhere. There is no authority which does not come from God. Therefore, we can encounter and recognize authority everywhere.

Thank God, there is a growing sense of recognizing authority in our midst. Among a group of three or four people, we can see authority there. This is a basic Christian lesson. Unfortunately, some people acknowledge only one person as the authority. This is submitting to a man, not really to authority. Find authority everywhere, and begin to fall into rank in relation to it. All this is voluntary, not something forced. For the characteristic of a Christian is not rebellion but submission; whereas the characteristic of Satan is rebellion. In case we encounter any command from the authority which is contradictory to basic Christian faith, then we should adopt the principle of "obeying God rather than man" (see Acts 5.29). Otherwise, let us learn to submit ourselves to authority.*

---

* Note: Messages given in Shanghai, January 1949.

OTHER TITLES AVAILABLE
From Christian Fellowship Publishers
By Watchman Nee

Basic Lesson Series
Volume 1 - A Living Sacrifice
Volume 2 - The Good Confession
Volume 3 - Assembling Together
Volume 4 - Not I, But Christ
Volume 5 - Do All to the Glory of God
Volume 6 - Love One Another

CD Rom — The Complete Works of Watchman Nee as Published by CFP

Aids to "Revelation"
Back to the Cross
A Balanced Christian Life
The Better Covenant
The Body of Christ: A Reality
The Character of God's Workman
Christ the Sum of All Spiritual Things
The Church and the Work
Come, Lord Jesus
The Communion of the Holy Spirit
The Finest of the Wheat - Volume 1
The Finest of the Wheat - Volume 2
From Faith to Faith
From Glory to Glory
Full of Grace and Truth - Volume 1
Full of Grace and Truth - Volume 2
Gleanings in the Fields of Boaz
The Glory of His Life
God's Plan and the Overcomers
God's Work
Gospel Dialogue
Grace for Grace
Interpreting Matthew
Journeying Towards the Spiritual
The King and the Kingdom of Heaven
The Latent Power of the Soul
Let Us Pray

The Life That Wins
The Lord My Portion
The Messenger of the Cross
The Ministry of God's Word
The Mystery of Creation
Powerful According to God
Practical Issues of This Life
The Prayer Ministry of the Church
The Release of the Spirit
Revive Thy Work
The Salvation of the Soul
The Secret of Christian Living
Serve in Spirit
The Spirit of Judgment
The Spirit of the Gospel
The Spirit of Wisdom and Revelation
Spiritual Authority
Spiritual Exercise
Spiritual Knowledge
The Spiritual Man
Spiritual Reality or Obsession
Take Heed
The Testimony of God
Whom Shall I Send?
The Word of the Cross
Worship God
Ye Search the Scriptures

By Stephen Kaung

Discipled to Christ
The Songs of Degrees - *Meditations on Fifteen Psalms*
The Splendor of His Ways - *Seeing the Lord's End in Job*

ORDER FROM:
11515 Allecingie Pkwy
Richmond, VA 23235

www.c-f-p.com